Birds That Came Back

Other books by John Gooders

Where to Watch Birds
Where to Watch Birds in Europe
How to Watch Birds
Wildlife Paradises
The Bird-Watcher's Book
The Second Bird-Watcher's Book
The Third Bird-Watcher's Book
A Day in the Country
Collins Bird Guide (with Stuart Keith)
Birds — A Survey of the Bird Families of The World
Wildlife Photography (with Eric Hosking)
Birds of the World (9 vols, Editor)
The Encyclopedia of Birds (7 vols, Editor)
The Bird Seeker's Guide
Finding Birds Around the World (with Peter Alden)
Collins British Birds

John Gooders

Birds That Came Back

ANDRE DEUTSCH

First published 1983 by
André Deutsch Limited
105 Great Russell Street London WC1

Printed in Great Britain by
Ebenezer Baylis and Son Ltd, Worcester

ISBN 0 233 97445 8

Contents

ILLUSTRATIONS

PREFACE

No 'History' could be compiled without drawing on the work of others, and the 'History of Birds' is no exception. *Birds That Came Back* is the result of thousands of man hours of effort by a comparatively small group of people determined to ensure that this country would offer a welcome return to birds that our grandfathers had shot out of existence. In many cases these people are named in the book itself, in others their wish for anonymity has been respected, and in some cases their achievements have been covered by time. But it is to this group of round-the-clock watchers, of secret-keepers, of plotters and enthusiasts that I and the birds owe the subject matter of this book.

Some of this band have written their own accounts of their adventures, of the elation and depression, of the toil and the rewards. Others have relied, somewhat modestly, on the writings of officials and administrators to tell their stories: to all I am permanently grateful. I have read their accounts with undiminished excitement, and attempted to pull them all together to give some sort of coherent account of the history of British birds over the last two centuries. Full bibliographical details of the books to which I refer in the text, are supplied in the list of 'Further Reading' on p. 177.

I have been fortunate enough to discuss many matters with friends, who pointed out a number of mistakes and errors. Nevertheless, the opinions expressed are entirely my own, as is the responsibility for any controversy they may arouse. I am, as ever, grateful to Hazel Cooper for making such a neat publisher-pleasing typescript from such a rag-bag of a manuscript.

INTRODUCTION

Nature is dynamic and rarely, if ever, achieves a balance. Species of animals and plants come and go; they are created and they become extinct. On a global canvas the dinosaurs were one of nature's most spectacular successes, reigning supreme for millions of years. They are still with us today, but their pre-eminence has been taken by the mammals. Such changes do not happen suddenly. Even at the level of individual species changes take time, thousands of years of time. Birds evolved, as far as we can tell, during the age of the dinosaurs. But the earliest birds that we know of have long since disappeared. They were right for their time, but they could not survive in competition with more sophisticated creatures and in changing times and conditions. No doubt the birds that we know today will (if they are allowed to survive man's incessant destructive force) evolve, become extinct, and be replaced by species better able to cope with conditions. This process is continuous, it is happening while I write and you read this book.

Most birds have a more or less continuous range or distribution. They may be confined to a particular habitat, that may itself be fragmented and partially isolated, but within their range they will occupy all suitable life zones. Should a bird species be divided into two (or more) distinct and separate populations, as, for instance, by a barrier of sea or ice, then these populations may, in their adaptations to their now distinct ranges, become differentiated. At first such differentiation may be sufficient only for them to merit sub-specific status, but sub-species are species in the making. Eventually the two populations may become so different in form or behaviour that they are incapable of interbreeding. At this stage their ranges may extend and even overlap.

Birds, like nature itself, continuously change. Some are young species expanding their range and growing in numbers. Others are in decline and subject to a contracting range. Both cases are the exceptions. Most birds increase and decrease, spread and contract according to a complex range of factors. At the heart of their range, that is in their most ideal circumstances, such changes may not be apparent. At the very edge of their range a small change in summer temperature may be sufficient to wipe out a whole population, or persuade it to withdraw. In Britain we are, by virtue of our geographical position, on the fringe of a large landmass, situated at the edge of the range of many species. Located on the edge of Europe we can, by definition, be at the very heart of the range only of species that occur on both sides of the Atlantic (or in the Atlantic and North Sea). We could thus reasonably expect to benefit from the dynamics of species populations; gaining a species here and losing another there. And indeed it would appear to be the case. So while we have cause for regret at the demise and loss of one former breeding bird, the chances are that another will simultaneously be colonizing for the first time.

All this would, in itself, make Britain a particularly interesting place to watch birds. However, the dynamic of nature is being progressively dominated by man. Man can, and has, destroyed individual species and drastically reduced populations of others. He has changed the landscape, turned forests into grasslands, grass-lands into scrub and scrub into desert. He has drained marshes, created lakes, enclosed intertidal wastes and covered huge areas with concrete. By destroying the great forests of the world it seems likely that he is even changing the climate. So man is progressively more important in determining which species of animals are most likely to prosper and which to decline and disappear. But though he may play a significant role in such evolutionary systems, this does not mean that man has a choice.

Significant as man may be as a force governing the range and distribution of birds and other animals, he too is subject to climatic and other natural forces. Indeed, it may be these natural forces, and the way that man reacts to them, that change the landscape for bird and animal populations. Thus, during the period of climatic amelioration that occupied most of the first half of the twentieth century, the growing season in the north was extended by two weeks, the crop-line shifted northwards by up to 100 miles in parts of Scandinavia, and lowland Scotland once more became farmable. As a result of such changes several birds were able to extend their range northwards, taking advantage of the new agricultural development. Lapwing, Rook, Starling and House Sparrow are cases in point.

It was during this warming period, with agriculture extending further northwards, that the ever-opportunistic House Sparrow moved along the Norwegian coast, apparently by hitching lifts on coastal steamers. In Siberia its colonization during the same period seems to have followed the railway lines — a sort of Soviet 'hobo' approach to colonization. In the Faeroe Islands it arrived by steamer in the 1930s and then used the well-established network of inter-island boats to spread through the archipelago.

Not all the extensions of range associated with warmer winters and extended growing seasons were at the specific level. In Scotland the Carrion Crow has moved northwards to displace the Hooded Crow, while the line of overlap and interbreeding between the two sub-species has similarly moved northwards.

While these extensions of range can be linked to an extension of agriculture, itself dependent on the amelioration of climate during the first half of this century, there have been other more direct effects on bird populations. The increase and range extension of the Gannet, for example, has been linked with a warmer Gulf Stream and increased winter supplies of coal fish around Shetland and elsewhere. Black-tailed Godwits have increased in Iceland since 1920. Little Gulls have prospered in Denmark and Holland, and Blackbirds have increased dramatically, becoming Britain's most abundant bird, and spread north to Shetland and the Faeroes as well as northwards in Scandinavia.

Alongside this extension of range northwards as a direct and indirect result of climatic amelioration, some species from the south have colonized Britain for the first time, while others in the north have declined or even disappeared. Snow Buntings certainly declined throughout the period 1914 to 1950, and Ptarmigan suffered a contraction of range that even attempted reintroductions could not quell. Dotterels disappeared from the Scottish border country along with Twite, and there have been declines in the populations of Ring Ouzel, Golden Plover and Wheatear. In recent years, since the 1950s, the increasing deterioration (that is cold weather) has led to an increase in several of these species, notably Snow Buntings, Ptarmigan, Dotterel and Twite.

At the same time new birds have colonized from the north for the first time during the past thirty or so years and it would be easy to correlate these with our more severe climate. Yet these same species were not with us during earlier periods of severe temperatures, so why should they be so now? The explanation may have something to do with weather during the spring migration, the mean summer or spring temperature, breeding populations of the species concerned in Scandinavia, or other factors. What is certain is that climatic change has, and will continue to have, a strong effect on the bird populations of these islands.

Birds That Came Back is the story of those species which were exterminated in historical times and which have since returned to breed with us once more. But it is also intended to record the other dramatic changes that have taken place in our bird fauna in recent times. To be set against the losses, there have been gains, though not all have been particularly welcome. There have been massive increases of some species, notably of gulls, Fulmar and Gannet, and catastrophic declines in species such as the Red-backed Shrike, Stone-curlew and Woodlark. There has been a near miss to the main title in the Wryneck, which was all but extinct in southern England, but which just held on long enough to see the colonization of Scotland by Scandinavian birds. Had the two events been separated by a few years then the Wryneck too would have qualified as a 'bird that came back'.

It is not our purpose to follow the changing fortunes of every one of the two hundred or so British breeding birds; that has been done admirably enough in Tim Sharrock's *Atlas of Breeding Birds in Britain and Ireland*. Instead, and keeping as near to the title as possible, we shall trace the history of birds that have become extinct and that have since returned to breed with us once more. Along the way we shall cover the birds that suffered a similar fate, but which for one reason or another have failed to make it back to Britain. A place must be found for the new colonists too, many of which may have bred here in the distant past, and several of which may be responding to similar pressures to those which have led others to make a return. Cetti's Warbler, for example, has spread across Europe to colonize Britain for the *first time*, while Savi's Warbler has followed the same course to make a *return* as a breeding bird. But for a fluke of history, Savi's too would have been greeted as a new colonist, not a recolonizer.

Attempts are continuing to reintroduce two further species that formerly bred with us, but which do so no more. In each case the chance of natural recolonization is remote, but the story of the present attempts to bring back the Great Bustard and White-tailed Eagle bears a remarkable similarity to that of the re-establishment of the once-extinct Capercaillie. The White-tailed Eagle is the only British bird to have become extinct as a breeder during the present century.

Of other birds that have so far failed to return, the Great Auk is extinct not only in Britain, but as a species throughout its former range. It is as dead as the Dodo, and just as unlikely to be seen again. But the Spoonbill bred in England and Wales until the seventeenth century and still does so in nearby Holland. Every year a handful of these magnificent birds set the watchers at Minsmere afrenzy by staying on into May and displaying. They have the potential to recolonize Britain as the Avocet did.

The Crane, too, bred with us until the sixteenth century and still exists in large numbers in Scandinavia. It is a migrant that occasionally reaches our shores and exceptionally may turn up in large numbers, as in the autumn of 1963. Their traditional migration route lies through southern Holland and Belgium on their way to winter quarters in central and southern Spain, well away from suitable breeding sites in Britain. But accidents do happen, and there is ample evidence that Scandinavian birds are finding our climate progressively more suited to their needs. Who knows, perhaps these splendid birds will one day return to breed with us after an absence of four hundred years.

These then are the lost birds: Spoonbill last bred in the seventeenth century and is still just a potential recolonist; Crane last found breeding in the sixteenth century and is an irregular straggler that could still win through. Added to these are the Great Bustard and White-tailed Eagle. Both of these are non-migratory and declining, and though they are highly unlikely to recolonize their former British haunts, they are both at present the subject of reintroduction schemes. Finally there is the now extinct Great Auk.

A further group of birds of concern to us are the irregular breeders, some of which, like the Hoopoe and Golden Oriole, are more or less annual and may be increasing. For these birds Britain lies right at the edge of their geographical range. A small change up or down in mean summer temperature may prelude either a strong colonization, or extinction. Totally erratic are those species that have bred only once or twice, more or less by accident. Into this category come the Black-winged Stilts that bred in Nottinghamshire in 1945; the Cambridgeshire Moustached Warblers of 1946; the Gull-billed Terns of Abberton Reservoir in 1950; the Bee-eaters of 1920 and 1955; and the Baillon's Crakes of 1858, 1866 and 1889. Then there are the most extraordinary breeding records of all — birds that were so way off course that to regard them as anything other than aberrant would be foolish. In 1888, following a massive eruption from their Siberian breeding grounds, Pallas's Sandgrouse bred in several parts of the country. There have been few irruptions since and the sad decline of the species in its native haunts makes further invasions highly unlikely. The breeding of a pair of Spotted Sandpipers in Scotland in 1975 can only be put into proper perspective when it is realized that these birds are natives of North America, three thousand miles off course; by the end of 1978 no more than forty-seven individuals had been recorded in the entire history of British ornithology.

Finally, among this group of irregular breeders we can class a variety of northern birds that in the coming years may join the ranks of others of similar origins that have colonized Britain. In this group we find the Great Northern Diver, first proved to breed in 1970 after a century or more of speculation. There is also the Whooper Swan, that breeds some years while not others and which has been tantalizing ornithologists for years. Bramblings have been doing the same, while the Bluethroat that bred in 1968 was the first and last so far. While several Scandinavian waders have established colonies for the first time in recent years, no such claims can be made for the Green Sandpiper, the last of our erratics. It bred in 1917 and 1959; perhaps it will do so again.

What then of the birds that have bred in Britain for the first time during the past hundred years or so, and which have consolidated their colonization or seem likely to do so? Some have come from the south, though recently the north has provided more new birds for our breeding list. The fantastic spread of the Collared Dove across Europe from its home in the Balkans during the present century is too well known to need but passing mention. In Britain it was first noted as recently as 1955, but within ten years was already regarded as a pest by the hotel keepers of the Isle of Thanet, where guests were complaining of being kept awake by the birds' incessant and penetrating calls. By the time I visited the Faeroes in 1978 they were well established in Torshavn, calling throughout the twilight of the brief arctic night. Next stop Iceland. Then on to the inhabitable parts of Greenland and thence to the New World? What the voracious Collared Dove will make of the grain-rich prairies remains a subject of conjecture: but since the demise of the Passenger Pigeon that once darkened the prairie skies in their millions, there has been a vacant niche for a pigeon in the heartland of America.

The Little Ringed Plover, that first bred at the partially-drained Tring Reservoirs in 1938, has since spread throughout England, taking advantage of the newly-created habitat provided by gravel pits. The Black Redstart arrived about the same time and similarly benefited from freshly-created habitats in consolidating its position. In this case it was the bomb sites of Central London that offered a home to the newcomer, though as redevelopment deprived the bird of this habitat it gradually shifted to industrial wasteground.

Also from the south came the Serin, which is still battling for its status as a regular British breeding bird after its initial colonization in 1967 and 1969. Similarly, the Firecrest has been struggling to maintain its toe-hold in southern England after its arrival from the Continent. It has enjoyed more success than the Serin, but its position still remains precarious. It is easily overlooked in forests full of Goldcrests. In contrast, Cetti's Warbler has arrived with a flourish. After spreading northwards across France during the 1950s this warbler was checked by the severe winters of 1962 and 1963. Its progress, however, did little more than falter. Though it was added to the British List in 1961, it remained a vagrant until 1972. It was then proved to breed in Kent and thereafter increased dramatically. By 1975 around fifty-six to fifty-eight males were singing in the Kent stronghold along the Stour Valley, while by 1978 perhaps as many as 178 pairs were breeding from Cornwall and Glamorgan through southern England to Kent, where no less than 107 singing males could be heard.

Two other birds with southern rather than northern affinities also began what may turn out to have been the early stages of a colonization. Mediterranean Gulls settled among the huge gullery at Needs Oar Point in Hampshire and happily hybridized with the local Black-headed Gulls as well as forming the occasional pure pair. Little Gulls bred at the Ouse Washes in 1975 and at a Norfolk site and the RSPB reserve at Fairburn Ings in Yorkshire in 1978.

Turning now to the north, there has been an extraordinary colonization of typically Scandinavian birds in recent years. Some were previously erratic breeders like the Whooper Swan, others were quite unexpected. The Snowy Owls that settled on Shetland in 1967 are a case in point. Formerly no more than an erratic winter visitor to the Scottish Highlands and Islands, an increasing regularity in Shetland led to breeding in each of the nine years between 1967 and 1975. Only the lack of a suitable male apparently prevents breeding today, for there are several females present every season. No less dramatic has been the arrival of breeding Shore Larks in 1972 and 1973; of Lapland Buntings in 1977 and 1978; of Temminck's Stints since 1969, after four previous attempts between 1934 and 1956; of Wood Sandpipers since 1959; of Goldeneyes since 1970; of Fieldfares since 1967; and of Redwings in the late 1950s.

Along with these northern colonists have come Wrynecks and Red-backed Shrikes to colonize new areas of Britain, just as their original populations were withdrawing from southern England. In 1978, for example, the southern Wryneck population was reduced to two males singing in Suffolk and another in Surrey. Meanwhile no less than eighteen sites were occupied in Scotland, with breeding proved in several. Though less dramatically, the Red-backed Shrike seems to be following the same pattern. Of a possible thirty-seven pairs in Britain, five were in Scotland, where Shrikes are becoming increasingly regular, the rest were in southern England where the species is in decline.

Other birds have become established breeders in these islands from a quite different source. The increasing popularity of bird gardens and collections has inevitably led to escapes, and the establishment of feral populations at various levels of self-sufficiency. Waterfowl are particularly easy to breed, but difficult to catch for pinioning. As a result, species as diverse as Mandarin Duck and Egyptian Goose have already been added to the British List as feral species. Populations of feral Golden and Lady Amherst's Pheasants are similarly recognized. These are, however, just the tip of the iceberg. Red-crested Pochards breed at Frampton, not far from the Wildfowl Trust's collection at Slimbridge. American Wood Duck, or Carolina Duck, breed at several places from southern England north to Cumbria. Ruddy Duck, another North American bird, breeds in the West Midlands and the Bristol area, having spread along the Severn Valley from its Slimbridge origins. Night-Herons breed in Edinburgh Zoo, but have flighted out to feed in the surrounding neighbourhood since 1950. Bob-white Quail live ferally around Minsmere (as if that area had not got enough rare birds) and Tresco. Reeves's Pheasants can be found in three widely-separated areas of Britain and are still being introduced on a significant scale in others. Rose-ringed Parakeets (misleadingly called 'Ring-necked' by altogether too many British ornithologists) started breeding ferally around the suburbs of London during 1969 and 1971 and have now spread as far as the south coast and to Westleton in Suffolk, where I saw one in August 1979. Budgerigars, perhaps the world's most commonly kept cage birds, had by 1975 established a thriving colony on the Isles of Scilly after their initial release in 1969, and there were also signs of success at a few spots in eastern England. Added to these are records of those species turned up during the great scouring of our countryside associated with the *Atlas* Project; these included Muscovy Duck along with Chinese and Barnacle Geese — no surprises there — but also Barbary Dove, Canary, Java Sparrow and, believe it or not, Pin-tailed Whydah. This species, in its native Africa south of the Sahara at least, is parasitic on various species of waxbills and cisticolas. Which species it chose in its probable British breeding is not disclosed.

These, then, are the species gained and lost over the past two hundred years or so. There remain those that were lost and which, of their own accord, have returned to breed with us once again. It is tempting to add 'unaided by man', but this would be both misleading and grudging of credit where it is due. Virtually every one of the returning species has benefited directly from human aid. Some have been deliberately provided with newly-created habitats; others have been guarded day and night as they attempted their earliest returns; all are protected by special penalties under the Bird Protection Acts.

I have intentionally left this special collection of birds till last so that their position does not over-emphasize their importance. The fact that we have had success with some species does not mean that we have not failed with others. That some birds have come back should not blind us to the fact that others, that never did become quite extinct, are still in a perilous position. Red Kites were all but extinct at the turn of the century; Montagu's Harriers seem destined to become so within the present decade. Dartford Warblers hover on the brink and the Woodlark seems certain to disappear sooner rather than later. It is against this, I hope sobering, background that I introduce the 'stars' of this book.

The first to return was the Marsh Harrier, which was absent from England between 1878 and 1926, save for a handful of attempted breedings, most of which ended in the birds being at worst 'collected' or at best robbed of their eggs. For part of this period Marsh Harriers continued to breed in Ireland, but even there they were extinct by 1917 and so were absent from every part of these islands for at least ten years. The Honey Buzzard, though perhaps never widespread, was certainly regular until 1911. It was then absent until 1923 and only became regular again in 1928. Thereafter a few pairs bred annually, though their whereabouts have always remained a widely-known 'secret'.

More spectacular was the return of the Avocet in 1947, after an absence of a hundred years. Not surprisingly it was this boldly-patterned and elegant wader that caught both the imagination and the headlines. The work of the RSPB in respect of the Avocet has been monumental: the effect of the Avocet success on this once-tiny Society has been no less dramatic. Black-tailed Godwits returned to breed under a cloak of secrecy on the wild Ouse Washes in 1952, after an absence of at least 120 years, to be followed by the Ruff in 1963 after forty-one years, and the Black Tern in 1966 for the first time since 1858.

Meanwhile Ospreys had returned to Scotland in 1955 and set up their eyrie near Loch Garten, where they are now watched (apparently unaware) by thousands of tourists each year. They had last bred in 1916 and had thus been extinct for forty years. Another raptor, the Goshawk, had formerly nested in England and Scotland until the 1880s but then disappeared until 1938, when up to three pairs returned to Sussex. Their whereabouts were a well-kept secret, known only to a handful of ornithologists and the inevitable egg collectors. Today this hawk has recolonized on a grand scale, mainly, no doubt, by escapes from the increasingly popular sport of falconry.

Only one of our select bunch is a passerine — Savi's Warbler. This does not mean that small birds are less likely to make comebacks, but rather that they were much more difficult to destroy in the first place. Though persecuted for its rarity during the brief period between its recognition as a species and its final demise, there can be little doubt that loss of habitat and perhaps a natural contraction of range were responsible for its disappearance from Britain. It returned in 1960 after an absence of just over a hundred years.

Finally there is the Kentish Plover, often listed, along with the White-tailed Eagle, as one of only two British birds to have become locally extinct during the present century. Officially the Kentish Plover did not breed between 1956 and 1979, but it is widely known that these birds returned to southern England and bred in the late 1970s.

These then are the *dramatis personae* of our story. In subsequent pages I shall follow their fortunes and try to determine the causes of their decline and final disappearance. I shall seek to explain the changes that made Britain into a more hospitable home and trace the story of their return and recolonization. In doing so I shall digress to discuss the fortunes of other birds, for this is a history of British birds, and history, as everyone knows, is either complex or bunkum.

Chapter One

Hunting and Shotguns

Britons were hunting birds before recorded history began. Cave dwellers of the Old Stone Age have left behind a mass of bones from which ornithologists have built up a picture of the birds of the period, or at least of the birds that these primitive peoples successfully hunted. Over sixty different species have been identified from bones found in Chudleigh Cave in Devon and over thirty from caves in the Wye Valley. At Jarlshof in Shetland forty-two birds have been identified from a late Bronze Age settlement, while in Clevedon in Somerset there are records of White-tailed Eagles, geese and duck, Heron, Cormorant, Swift and many others. Chudleigh, however, provides us with the best evidence of the hunting ability of the Britons of the Upper Pleistocene, as well as of the changes that have taken place in the British avifauna during the past 150,000 years. These hunters managed to take Hazel Grouse (extinct in Britain well before historical times), Little Owl (extinct and now reintroduced), as well as species as varied as Snowy Owl and Wren.

The first British farmers appeared much later in Neolithic times, about 3,000 to 1,500 BC and though they did not change the landscape in any radical way, we know that they hunted Crane and Dalmatian Pelican – both now extinct as breeding birds.

The art of 'fowling' for seabirds and their eggs, practised in Britain as recently as the 1930s and still continued by the men of Ness, in the Outer Hebrides, who enjoy a licensed exemption from wildlife conservation legislation to take young Gannets from the island of Sula Sgeir, can be traced back to the Bronze Age. The site at Jarlshof shows that seabirds formed an important part of the economy, but that divers, Shag, Curlew and even the diminutive Storm Petrel and now extinct Great Auk, were all taken.

Excavations at Glastonbury in Somerset reveal that the inhabitants of a once-substantial village not only raided the local bird-rich marshes for duck, swans, Bittern, White-tailed Eagle and Kite, but also took Dalmatian Pelican and even organized trips to seabird islands, presumably in the Bristol Channel, to collect Shearwaters.

The coming of the Romans brought to this 'barbaric' isle not only their well-known skills of road and palace building, but also a passion for domesticating birds. The introduction of the Pheasant is generally attributed to the invading legions, but they also brought domestic pigeons and doves, and even trained Ravens to talk.

The so-called Dark Ages have typically produced little evidence of birds, though a lake-dwelling population at Lagore in Co. Meath clearly took advantage of the rich avifauna they found on their doorstep. Wildfowl of perhaps sixteen distinct species were consumed along with divers, Cormorant, Heron, Crane and White-tailed Eagle. The effect of such hunting on the population of British birds can only be guessed at, but it was probably minimal. Slings, arrows and traps may be effective in the right hands, but they are hardly weapons of mass destruction. What really changed the avifauna were the changes wrought on our countryside by farmers.

During the Iron Age and subsequent occupation by the Romans, farming grew progressively more important and radically changed the bird life of these islands. From some forty million acres in the Neolithic Period the axes of stone, bronze and iron halved the amount of woodland by the end of the Roman occupation. This acreage was halved yet again by the time of the Norman Conquest. The onslaught continued so that by the mid-eighteenth century Britain's woodlands were reduced to no more than two million acres, an all-time low. Recent plantings have pushed the total up to three million acres; but this remains only a tiny fraction of what existed in pre-Roman times. The effects of such drastic clearances, particularly on the larger and more obvious species such as the birds of prey, can easily be imagined. It is a theme to which we shall return.

Direct destruction of our birds has been stepped up by a progressive command of ever more powerful weapons. The first great step forward, if that is not an inappropriate term, was the introduction of falconry. The sport is generally regarded as having reached England about 860 AD, but there is some evidence from Yorkshire of Bronze Age falconry nearly 3,000 years earlier. Certainly it originated in China even earlier still.

By the time of Henry VIII falconry was a serious sport and practised by a wide range of classes. The ability to fly a 'hawk' at other birds opened up the potential for year-round killing of a wide variety of birds and already there was some concern about over-hunting of large prey such as Herons and Cranes. No one can say how many falcons were flown or to what effect on the British avifauna. It is, however, certain that the destruction was as nothing compared with what was soon to follow.

Gunpowder, quaintly called Black Powder, was discovered in 1250, though it may have been known to the ancient Chinese and perhaps even used in Europe as rocket fuel as early as the tenth century. Whatever the historical facts, this mixture of 74.6 percent saltpetre, 13.5 percent charcoal and 11.9 percent sulphur was the only explosive available until nitroglycerin and nitrocellulose were discovered in the mid-nineteenth century.

At first its use was strictly limited by the nature of the mixture and it was not until the early fourteenth century that it was used in guns. These first firearms were cumbersome to say the least and required two or more men to use them. An eight- to twelve-inch solid barrel of brass, sometimes iron, was mounted on a five- to eight-feet long handle. The muzzle-loading technique of a measure of powder held down by a wad and followed by a missile, usually a ball, was to remain standard for centuries. It was ignited by pushing a red-hot wire through a small touch hole. Such primitive instruments may have frightened the enemy, but they certainly lacked the speed of the contemporary long bow and could have been of only restricted use for hunting. Birds had little to fear as long as the state of development remained at this level.

The potentiality of such a weapon, however, attracted many a bright mind and soon the firing mechanism was improved by the use of a match of hemp soaked in saltpetre. Barrels became longer and stocks shorter. Curved stocks that overcame the problem of recoil were designed in the 1490s in France, and about the same time the use of a pan for powder outside the touch hole was introduced. The matchlock, a system for covering the ignition match, originated between 1425 and 1450 allowing a man to fire a gun on his own. The flintlock was invented in France between 1610 and 1615 and by 1650 this vastly improved system had replaced all others.

Plan of the Sporting Case.

A plan of an early nineteenth-century sporting case, housing an array of weapons suitable for exterminating virtually any form of wildlife the sportsman might encounter in these islands.

Not all attention was devoted to the igniting system however. Experiments with cartridges had been going on since the second half of the sixteenth century, and paper cartridges were used in the United States as early as 1650. These involved biting the tip off the cartridge, priming the pan, and pushing the rest down the muzzle. Such cartridges were in standard use in Europe by the early eighteenth century.

The flintlock remained standard until 1816, when an Englishman living in America, one Joshua Shaw, invented the percussion lock. By 1825 it had been widely accepted and was standard on new guns. Fortunately old flintlocks could be converted to the new system. Flintlock guns had been developed to a high level of sophistication, but they always remained unreliable in wet or windy weather.

Two final elements of sophistication evolved about the same time in the mid-nineteenth century. Muzzle loading was replaced by breech loading, and cartridges with their own ignition system were introduced. The latter were first produced by the famous Smith and Wesson Company in 1856, with a rim-fire system, only to be replaced by the modern centre-fire system, invented by the Englishman Charles Lancaster in 1852 and improved by Pottet in France in 1857. A Mr Boxer later improved this system by introducing a separate central section to the cartridge, which crushed easily against the firing compound. So the modern cartridge was perfected.

Throughout this lengthy development special sporting guns loaded with shot rather than a single ball had taken their toll of wildlife, including birds. However, the changes in the second half of the nineteenth century were to say the least dramatic. Between 1860 and 1900 the muzzle-loading hammer gun was replaced by breech-loading, self-ejecting, hammerless guns, often with a single trigger to work both barrels. The modern shot gun had arrived. Choke boring had been introduced, barrels were made of fine steels and reduced in length. So that while fowling pieces of the seventeenth century could spread an even pattern of shot, it was the second half of the nineteenth century that saw the development of sporting guns to the sophistication of modern weapons. Shotguns have changed little over the last hundred years and seem unlikely to do so in the foreseeable future.

With the development of the sporting gun birds became increasingly vulnerable. Large and naturally scarce species such as the Great Bustard succumbed by the middle of last century, while others struggled on in ever-decreasing numbers until they, too, finally disappeared. The assault was twofold. Birds were pursued by collectors and by sportsmen with an interest in natural history, intent on building up a collection of specimens mounted and boxed in glass cases to adorn their libraries and studies. For these gentlemen of leisure the rarer the bird the greater the desire to kill it, for ornithology at that time was a matter of collecting rather than watching and noting.

The other assault was less directly concerned with the birds, but was perhaps even more destructive. The sport of shooting developed alongside the shotgun. In *Toxophilus* published in 1545, Roger Ascham treats archery as the main sport and wildfowl as the main quarry; the shotgun receives a mere mention. By 1621 in Gervase Markham's *Hunger's Prevention or The Whole Arte of Fowling*, the gun could be referred to as the 'fowling-piece', though the serious hunter still used the crossbow as his main weapon. The introduction of the flintlock soon after Markham's treatise had appeared, clearly marked a turning point in the history of shooting. By 1686 Richard Blome in *The Gentleman's Recreation* was able to advise on differing bores and barrel lengths for differing quarry, and even to recommend shooting flying quarry, with a spaniel to pick up, as the most fashionable form of hunting.

Until 1760 the most popular form of hunting remained a man, a gun and a dog out walking and stalking. Then came the Enclosure Acts and with them hedgerows. Common land became private property and so did the birds and rabbits that inhabited it. So the peasant who was used to eking out a living with a little snaring and trapping was quickly turned into a poacher and law breaker. Naturally game stocks had to be protected and it was not long before the best of the poachers were employed as gamekeepers and provided with their own cottage well away from their village origins. The war against so-called 'vermin' started at this time, about 1780.

It was not, however, until the breech-loader and cartridge systems were perfected in the mid-nineteenth century that hunting changed radically. Then quite suddenly the armoury was available to allow rapid shooting and reloading and all at once Grouse and Partridges could be driven over standing guns instead of being walked up by an individual. Previously an expert shot could get up to the forty-four Grouse in a day obtained by Squire Osbaldeston. On 30 August 1888 Lord Walsingham killed 1,070 – a total change had taken place. A similar change took place in Partridge shooting, where the old record of the redoubtable Colonel Hawker of fifty-six birds in a day was smashed on 8 September 1876 by Maharajah Dulup Singh with 780.

A Victorian shooting party posed with guns at the ready. Those of the two gentlemen on the right are correctly broken, those of the younger men on the left are not.

Then, again quite suddenly, the Pheasant, for so long both rare and ignored, was discovered as a gamebird. Not without some degree of justification can the years from 1880 to 1914 be called 'The Pheasant Era'. Huge numbers of birds were reared specifically to be shot, with a record of 3,945 Pheasants shot in a single day. Pheasant densities were prodigious, and over-stocking and disease rife. As Eric Parler writes in his *Shooting Days*:

> Every creature which was not game was for that reason the enemy of game, and so was to be shot or trapped or otherwise put out of a world which should only fitly contain partridges, pheasants, hares, rabbits and gamekeepers. His traps befoul the woods, the hazels which he hung with stoats were horrors known afar.

This, then, was the golden age of shooting and the dark age of conservation. Huge numbers of birds, particularly birds of prey, were shot and trapped and several species were brought to the very verge of extinction.

The gamekeeper of the time, as is still, to a certain extent, the case today, knuckled his forelock and did his duty. As gamekeeping has always been a somewhat ill-defined occupation, only the test of

A GOOD DAY'S WORK IN THE COVERS—COUNTING THE BAG

A print dated 1882 shows the results of a day's work, with beaters and bearers standing aside. Most of the bag are pheasants, but there are hares, duck and two owls on display.

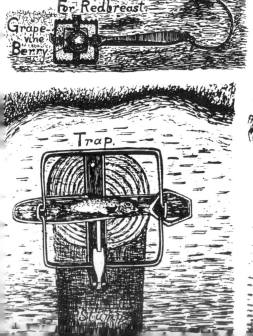

No bird was immune from the nineteenth century traps. Redbreast, Kingfisher and Heron all had devices invented for their destruction, so that they could be preserved in a glass case.

results could prove whether or not the gamekeeper was doing his job, or skiving off to while away his day in self-indulgence. When it comes to shooting, results may vary as much as the farmer's harvest. A wet spring that reduces hatching success may be a disaster, so a simple totalling of the 'bag' at the end of the season is no indication of gamekeeper efficiency, a fact known even to the great landlord sportsmen of the nineteenth century. No! The only means by which an efficient gamekeeper could prove his worth was by maintaining a hefty gibbet. No doubt a well-stocked gibbet was evidence of a hard-working gamekeeper, but it had little to do with the quantity of game available to shoot, and still less with the health, or otherwise, of his beat. The hanging corpses of Buzzards, Kestrels, Peregrines, Marsh Harriers and others may have impressed the boss, but an elementary knowledge of the food of such species would have convinced anyone of the wasted time, money and effort involved.

It was the shotgun that created this new approach to our countryside – it provided the wherewithal for the sport and was one of the gamekeeper's main means of destruction. Shotgun broken over the arm, dog at his heels, he would set off on his rounds every morning. By breakfast time his bag might be full of vermin such as stoats and weasels, fox and squirrel, birds of prey, Crows and Jays, with perhaps the odd rabbit thrown in for good measure and to eke out the meagre wages he received for his butchery. But he also had at his disposal a whole battery of traps and snares with which to continue his onslaught. Spring traps, pole traps, nets and the use of poisoned baits made his job both easier and more certain. But so important was the shoot, as evidence the iniquitous Game Laws, that even man traps were allowed by law and the punishments for poaching included deportation to one of the colonial penal settlements as far away as Australia. The fact that today the poacher is regarded as something of a folk hero instead of a thief is at least partly due to the unreasonable laws of the last century.

The increase in gamekeepers in the first half of the nineteenth century was phenomenal. Some even had to take an oath similar to that sworn by gamekeepers on the Marquis of Bute's Argyll estates: '. . . finally I shall use my best endeavours to destroy all birds of prey with their nests wherever they can be found. So help me God.' A couple of examples will help to show the extent of the destruction

An unusual and remarkably enlightened notice issued to his gamekeepers by Lord Barnard, offering some hope to a variety of birds and other wildlife that found refuge on his estate.

that afflicted birds of prey in mid-nineteenth-century Britain.

In Glen Garry in the three years 1837 to 1840 destruction included (Pearsall quoted in Meinertzhagen – *Pirates and Predators*) 98 Peregrines, 78 Merlins, 462 Kestrels, 285 Buzzards, 3 Honey Buzzards, 15 Golden Eagles, 27 White-tailed Eagles, 18 Ospreys, 63 Goshawks, 275 Kites and 68 miscellaneous (mostly Hen?) harriers – a total of no less than 1,372 diurnal birds of prey. That such occurrences were not isolated is evidenced by an almost identical number of victims, including no less than 171 adult eagles, on the Duchess of Sutherland's estates between 1831 and 1834 (Wolley 1902 and Ritchie 1920 in Bijleveld – *Birds of Prey in Europe*, 1974). Can it then be wondered at that one after another birds with hooked bills became rare? No population of slow-producing birds could stand such an onslaught.

However, once their numbers had been reduced so as to make the survivors both elusive and scarce there was little need for the gamekeeper to keep up the persecution, though no doubt he continued to shoot any raptor that came his way out of habit. Now it was the turn of the collector.

Chapter Two

The Age of the Collector

All collectors have something in common whether they collect paintings, stamps, train numbers or even, dare I say, sightings of birds. The rarer the subject the more valuable it becomes, the more it is prized, the harder it is sought. The lengths that an individual will go to acquire a Van Gogh are paralleled by those to which a philatelist will go for a 'Post Office' Mauritius Penny, a train spotter will travel to see a 4-8-4, or a tick lister to see a Ross's Gull.

Roped down from the cliff top, this nineteenth-century collector secures a young eagle from a most improbably sparse nest on a Scottish Highland crag.

Imagine then the effect if the collection is of stuffed and mounted specimens of British birds, or a tray of blown eggs? The rarer the bird the greater the kudos, satisfaction, pride, achievement and, ultimately, even money involved. So once the gamekeepers had done their work a much smaller, but if anything more dedicated, army moved in.

Birds, already shot out to danger point, were pursued with avid enthusiasm by a highly competitive group of doctors, parsons and gentlemen of leisure. Their aim, as with most devoted collectors, was the complete coverage of every rare species. Thus a stuffed and mounted skin was only a beginning. Ideally they required a male, female, young and at least one full clutch of eggs plus a nest. Having shot one member of a pair they would lie in wait for its mate to return to the nest, collect it (a polite euphemism), climb the tree to take young and/or eggs and then set to with saw to acquire even the largest of nests. The complete collection would then be expertly mounted and placed in a glass-boxed diorama with remarkable attention to detail and great expertise. Certainly these nineteenth-century taxidermists developed the art to a fine point. Their work makes their modern-day equivalents in Mediterranean countries look the hacks they are.

E.T. Booth, for example, gives a very graphic account of his adventures in search of birds in his book *Rough Notes*. To the present-day reader it seems a diary of senseless slaughter, but there is much natural history and learning buried away among the collecting. Booth, like his contemporaries, was a good ornithologist. Born in a different time he might have pursued his quarry with field glasses and notebook, or more likely with a 35mm camera and telephoto lens. When fashion changed most collections were broken up and sold off, bequeathed to a museum, or left neglected in an attic to be devoured by insects. Booth's collection remains intact, and to visit it at the Dyke Road Museum in Brighton is to enter into another age. One is cast back over a hundred years as one walks past case after case crammed full of remarkably life-like birds, birds in every plumage and attitude. The atmosphere is nineteenth century and there is no monument to the pastimes of the Victorian gentleman to compare with it.

Booth and his fellow collectors were great travellers and did not confine their attentions purely to British birds. Some scoured

Europe and added greatly to our knowledge of continental birds. R.B. Lodge vividly describes his travels in southern Europe in a now unfortunately rare and expensive volume *Bird Hunting Through Wild Europe*, which is on my desk as I write. It is a handsome little book with spine and cover decorated in typical Victorian fashion. The spine boasts a gold-embossed figure of a field camera and tripod, the front cover a portrait of a hunter in plus-fours, puttees and a bush hat with a gun in one hand and a 'collected' vulture over his shoulder. My particular copy has the emblem of the Glasgow and West of Scotland Society for the Prevention of Cruelty to Animals embossed on the back. The inside cover has the book plate of that Society awarding first prize to one Fred S. Bell for 'Essay on "The Duty of Mankind to the Lower Animals" May 1915'. Whether the Society chose this particular book as a warning to its prizewinner of the evils of mankind seems doubtful; but it is a strange choice.

Lodge set out to photograph and collect his way through Spain and the Balkans with remarkable dedication, apparently oblivious of hardship. The openness with which he summarizes '... a good day's work ... One egg of Bonelli's Eagle, two eggs of Griffon Vulture, and two eggs of Egyptian Vulture, constituted a good day's takings, without reckoning the Goldfinches' and other small eggs we had picked up accidentally on our way' shows the attitude of the day. He goes on to describe the taking of a Short-toed Eagle's egg and the accidental smashing of a second (unusual) while the sawn-off nest was being lowered to the ground. He describes his double-barrelled .410 as a mistake — too small for large birds and too powerful for smaller ones — 'the bird was generally knocked to bits and spoiled as a specimen'. In Albania '... I shot four Little Stints', '... a Reeve was shot out of a flock on April 25 ...', '... there is a supposed sub-species [of the Jackdaw] in Macedonia [so] I preserved the skins of nearly a dozen in case ...', and finally 'the fishermen ... did not regard the Pelicans ... as rivals ... but had a friendly regard for them and were quite unwilling for any of them to be shot'.

So throughout 'Wild Europe' Lodge continued his slaughter and egg collecting. Through the great wilderness of the Coto Doñana in southern Spain he roughed it in peasant shacks, over fifty years before modern British ornithologists organized a 'path-finding' expedition. He was in the Danube delta, Albania, Yugoslavia and Hungary at more or less the same time and opens one chapter with one of those endearing asides soon to seem particularly inept. Though it has nothing to do with birds, I cannot resist quoting it:

> Early in April 1906 I found myself in Sarajevo, a place the very existence of which . . . I had been profoundly ignorant a few weeks before . . . the capital of Bosnia . . . is not a place which makes much stir in the world, and it would be easy to go through life and never hear of it or see any reference to it.

Less than ten years later Sarajevo was to be etched on the minds of a whole generation, and have a place in history out of all proportion to its importance.

Lodge was typical of his day. He was dedicated to birds and made many significant observations in his travels. He was not a simple hunter-collector, but a man of culture and refinement, as intent on observing and photographing birds as he was on collecting their skins and eggs.

The First World War was something of a watershed. Though the laws of bird protection did not change, social attitudes did. The collector-hunter virtually disappeared. In the 1920s collecting was still important, but the aim was not to amass an impressive array of mounted specimens, but to prove scientifically the occurrence of a particular bird. Thus a rare wanderer to our shores could expect an explosive welcome, but scarce and rare breeders found a degree of peace they had not enjoyed for over a hundred years. Not that the search for and 'proof' of the existence of rare wanderers was anything new. Such vagrants had enjoyed a special place throughout the 'golden age' of collecting, for though rare breeding birds had been highly prized, the addition of a new bird to the 'British List' had always been one of the pinnacles of a lifetime's work in the field of ornithology.

All mounted specimens had a commercial value in an age in which no parlour was complete without its domed stuffed bird. To the collectors, however, a British-taken specimen was worth more than an imported one, and the rarer the bird the higher its cash value. What could be more valuable than the actual specimen on which a particular species had been admitted to the 'British List'? Not surprisingly, and to misquote Lord Acton, 'cash corrupts, and absolutely large amounts of cash corrupt absolutely'.

By the early 1900s the price of a specimen new to Britain was extraordinary, and the second, third, fourth, and so on specimens were valued in proportion. A thriving business soon grew up based on the Sussex seaside resort of Hastings and the shop of a particular taxidermist named Bristow. Over a period of several years a large number of species were added to the British List from specimens collected in the Hastings area, while the number of first-degree rarities (species that had occurred on only a handful of occasions) was truly staggering. Virtually without exception these birds found their way to Bristow's shop and were sold to prominent collectors of the time. Some were collected by ornithologists, but a great many were taken by local men and gamekeepers who (apparently) shot any interesting bird they came across. Bristow explained to the rightly sceptical Harry Witherby, doyen of British ornithologists, that he had to buy all sorts of common birds from his band of field scourers in order to keep up the supply of the unusual which he could sell.

It would seem (superficially at least) quite reasonable that a place on the south coast should receive more continental visitors than, say, a location in Scotland; and that the promontory of Dungeness should act as a landing point for such vagrants. But many of Bristow's birds were collected well inland and Dungeness, now the site of a well-watched bird observatory, has never done anywhere near as well again. For five years I had a cottage at Staplecross, some six miles inland from Hastings, yet I never saw anything rarer than a solitary Goshawk and a spring passage Ring Ouzel. Yet Staplecross and its neighbourhood produced an endless string of rarities in just a few years at the beginning of the century.

I could write (others have) a book on Bristow and the Hastings rarities, for it has been as significant to British ornithology as the Piltdown hoax was to British anthropology. Though the validity of some records has been argued at length, and no doubt the good have gone down with the bad, science demands acceptance only of records that are totally validated and not subject to question. There can be no doubt that many of the records from the Hastings area during this period are false and that many so-called British-taken specimens were shipped in (even on ice) from abroad.

The point of the Bristow Affair is that it shows both the mentality of contemporary collectors, and the value that a particular specimen could command. As a result of the exposure by *British Birds* magazine in 1962, six species were deleted from the British List based, as they were, on specimens taken only in the Hastings area during the period in question. Though there have been rumours, there is no positive evidence that other taxidermists in other parts of the country were involved in similar wheeler-dealing — though it would be surprising if Bristow was the only taxidermist guilty of such deceit.

If bird skins were so easy to pass off as 'British-taken', imagine the dealing and subterfuge that must have prevailed in the egg market. Collecting birds' eggs is a natural pastime of boyhood that, thank heaven, most of us get over by the time we argue our way out of short trousers. In the last century collecting eggs had at least some purpose — to show variation in size, colour and pattern within the clutch. What is more, the availability of a plentiful supply of material has been of great benefit in facilitating comparison, for example, between eggshell thickness today and in a pre-pesticide era. Nevertheless the amassing of private collections, often featuring a large series of clutches of scarce species, could not be justified in this way for very long.

Collecting eggs was simply a passion that some schoolboys never grew out of. It was, in its later stages, window-dressed with the pseudo-scientific title of oology, but it remained collecting for collecting's sake and a curiously British complaint. In America it is virtually unknown, on the Continent it never really caught on. In Britain it remains one of the most significant problems faced by conservationists and has led to the secrecy with which the whereabouts of certain birds have been cloaked to the present day. Between 1843 and the end of the century Ospreys bred at Loch an' Eilean in Speyside on twenty-four occasions. Their eggs were taken no less than fifteen times. Some seventy-five to a hundred pairs of Hobbies nest in England each year, yet it would be surprising if more than half managed to hatch their eggs. Golden Eagles, too,

Boys will be boys. These lads have taken nest, eggs and chicks, but are clearly delighted and may even have a sense of wonder at their prize.

have been robbed ruthlessly over the years, and any bird that attempts to breed for the first time has to face an army of shell hunters.

Like the specimen collectors, many of these egg-collectors were excellent bird-watchers and knew as much about their birds as any ornithologist. They met regularly at their own societies and clubs, showed off their most recent acquisitions and talked, no doubt, of the adventure they had enjoyed in their pursuit. To my knowledge I have met only a handful of egg collectors all of whom have, for one reason or another, given up the chase. One is a good friend who still takes every opportunity presented to go a-bush tapping in his search for nests — though he is careful in his searching and leaves the nest as he finds it . . . complete with contents. It was this friend who introduced me to his oological guru of yesteryear, he, in turn, invited me only a few years ago to see his collection.

Drawer after drawer was withdrawn from the beautifully-constructed mahogany cabinet, laid on the bed and the glass removed for inspection. Each drawer contained a series of symmetrically-placed hollows (quasi-nests) in which nestled the clutches that years of pursuit had brought. Some were plain, others quite beautiful. Some species varied amazingly, others were virtually 'factory-produced' replicas one of another. My eye was taken by a series of perhaps twenty clutches of Golden Eagle, then by an even larger number of Hobbies. There were Peregrines, harriers, Buzzards, Sparrowhawks, Kestrels and even Red Kites.

Personally, I have never been attracted either by birds' eggs or by their nests, but I was impressed by the sheer volume and quality that a single egger had acquired over a lifetime of collecting. All of these eggs, all these could-have-been-birds, were taken before the 1954 Protection of Birds Act put an end to legal egg collecting. No doubt the taking of this collection had a negligible effect on the populations of the birds concerned. Equally, there can be no doubt that the vast army of egg collectors who scoured Britain in the nineteenth and early part of the twentieth century did reduce the bird populations of several species. This is especially true of the rarer birds of prey, species that were also having to contend with the merciless extermination campaign waged by gamekeepers and the equally avid attentions of skin collectors. All three factors combined to reduce the population of several birds to the point of, and to actual, extinction as British breeding birds.

By 1898 Marsh Harriers had been finally eliminated from their last stronghold among the marshes of Norfolk, did not breed for several years, and thereafter only irregularly. Montagu's Harriers were down to three pairs and Hen Harriers had been eliminated everywhere save for Orkney and the Outer Hebrides. The White-tailed Eagle, from a position of numerical superiority to the Golden Eagle, was reduced to virtual extinction by 1900, with the last known nest in Skye in 1916. The same year saw the last Scottish Ospreys breed on an island in Loch Loyne. Golden Eagles, too, reached their lowest ebb about the turn of the century, having disappeared from region after region during the preceding two hundred years. A similar story can be told of the Buzzard, though both it and the Golden Eagle still survived in good numbers. The Goshawk, probably always confined in a genuine wild state to Scotland, was no more than an irregular breeder, but it, too, had disappeared completely by 1883. In contrast the Red Kite was, at one time, one of the most familiar of all British birds. It was common even over the streets of London, though it had disappeared there by the end of the eighteenth century. In the century that followed, it ceased to breed in county after county, so that by 1900 it was one of our rarest birds. No more than a dozen survived in a remote area of central Wales, where stringent efforts were made to protect it from both skin and egg collectors. The Honey Buzzard, though always scarce, was probably a regular breeder in the early part of last century, but it, too, was sought by collectors and by 1870 occurred only erratically.

Among British birds of prey only the falcons seem to have held their own through the persecution of the nineteenth century. That they were subject to similar pressures to the other raptors cannot be doubted, for they are among the most common species to be found mounted for decoration in old cases in 'antique' shops. Yet somehow Peregrine, Hobby, Merlin and Kestrel, together with the Sparrowhawk, managed to hang on in something approaching their former numbers. The Hobby was, as we have seen, a favourite target for egg collectors, but the systematic robbing together with the direct efforts of gamekeepers probably did no more than keep the population stable and prevent the spread to otherwise suitable areas. Peregrines, too, were sought by collectors, but their predominantly coastal habits did not bring them into daily contact with gamekeepers, and their population at the turn of the century was certainly healthy. For all we know there may have been a

A patented trap of the last century to catch small birds alive for the cage bird trade. The fashion of keeping colourful songsters in the house is still prevalent in southern Europe today.

decline in Merlin, Kestrel and Sparrowhawk, but strong populations survived the onslaught. Their turn was to come later from an even more potent source — the pesticides of the 1950s and 1960s.

Being large and naturally scarce species, birds of prey are the more obvious examples of species that suffered during the great age of destruction that ended with the First World War, but they are not the only ones. Owls, though protected by their nocturnal proclivities, were shot by gamekeepers and collectors alike, and the Barn Owl must be one of the most common of stuffed birds left as a domed legacy from that dark century.

Even small birds were not immune. Just as the freshly-urbanized population of southern Europe enjoy a passion for caged birds to brighten their homes, so did the nineteenth-century British keep Goldfinches, Linnets and other songsters to remind them of a recently lost rural past. The numbers of birds netted to be sold in the street markets of London's East End and elsewhere, were enormous, but though the effect on the populations of the species concerned remains unknown, it was probably not significant.

Much more important were the changes being wrought on the landscape of Britain. Historians of recent times have made much of the so-called 'agricultural revolution' of the late eighteenth and early nineteenth century, following on the heels of the contemporary Enclosure Acts. Individuals such as 'Turnip' Townshend, Thomas Coke and others certainly did change the nature of agricultural practice, but other economic historians are quick to point out that there was a similar revolution in the sixteenth century, and Sir John Clapham is famed for, among other things, diagnosing an agricultural revolution as early as the thirteenth century. Whatever the facts, there is no doubting the progressive changes that have affected the countryside of Britain over the last two thousand years. By the mid-eighteenth century old common lands were being converted to neatly hedged fields at what would have been an alarming pace, had there been anyone other than the dispossessed to be alarmed. Scrub and wood were destroyed to create that pattern of patchwork fields that we now take to be so typical of our countryside, and the destruction of which so concerns us today.

Alongside the enclosures and changing system of agriculture there was an ever-increasing demand for more land. Wasteland, such as heath and marsh, was continually being taken under the plough. Thomas Coke is famous for converting the wasteland of his Norfolk estate to fertile agricultural land between 1734 and 1759 by spreading marl over the sandy soil. His example was followed by others. At the same time ditches were dug and embankments raised to drain marshes throughout the land. Most notable of such projects was the draining of the Fens under the direction of the famous Dutch engineer Cornelius Vermuyden. Starting in 1630, the courses of the Ouse and Nene were altered from meandering streams connecting a maze of marshes to straight dykes with sluices and safety valves known at the time as 'Levels' and today called 'Washes'. Huge areas of fen were converted to rich agricultural land that quickly became the most productive region of Britain. At Wicken Fen we can still see a remnant of the old landscape, artificially maintained by careful manipulation of water levels as an island above the shrinking agricultural land that surrounds it. There can be little doubt that the marshes and scrub, reedbeds and pools were once the home of a remarkably rich avifauna, a landscape where Marsh and Montagu's Harriers, Bitterns and Bearded Tits, Ruffs and Black-tailed Godwits thrived. By draining this area, huge numbers of birds were dispossessed and their populations declined to the level where they became a major attraction to the collectors. So these species, along with Savi's Warbler and the Avocet, were put under pressure and ultimately exterminated.

By one means or another, the bird population of these islands had, by 1914, reached an all-time low. Gamekeepers, skin collectors and oologists had exterminated species after species, but their work had been massively aided by a less direct but by no means less effective destruction of habitats. The pace of change has not slackened during the twentieth century: only man's attitudes have changed.

Chapter Three

The Peace of War and After

By 1914 events in the little town of Sarajevo, described by R.B. Lodge in 1906 as insignificant and likely to remain so, had changed the history of the world. The assassination of the Grand Duke Ferdinand plunged the western world into the war to end all wars during which millions were killed and a significant part of Europe was laid to waste. Its effects, especially concerning the position and role of Britain in the world, are still with us today. From a wildlife viewpoint, however, the Great War was far from being the disaster it was in human terms. From town and village, city and hamlet, the most active and fit young men were shipped to the trenches of Flanders and France, where those who were not killed or maimed were tied down for four tedious years. Virtually the whole population of British gamekeepers ended up in the trenches. The collectors were there too, though perhaps in slightly more comfortable circumstances. Suddenly the birds had a respite, and they responded accordingly. Over the four years of war, plus the years of readjustment and depression that followed, rare and scarce birds were for the first time in a century allowed to get on with their lives in peace. As a result the populations of several species made a rapid recovery.

After the war things gradually returned to normal though, it is a cliché to say, they would never be the same. Nor would they. The days of a leisured class that could devote its time to natural history had gone. Gone too had the fashion of collecting skins and of decorating the home with cases and domes of stuffed birds. The bottom fell out of the plume market which, though it had little effect on British birds, save for the Great Crested Grebe which had been drastically reduced in numbers, seriously affected many bird species throughout the world. Some gamekeepers got back to work, but large estates were broken up and the record bag era had passed. Now shooting was for profit not leisured guests. Farmers were profit-conscious and aware of the damage caused to crops by over-population of gamebirds. Egg collectors were soon up to their usual tricks — but the populations of many of our birds were never

In summer the Great Crested Grebe sports beautiful nuptial plumes.
Though the nineteenth-century sportsman would have shot them anyway,
it was the plume hunters who really decided the fate of this bird.

again to sink as low as they had prior to 1914.

The frivolity of the 1920s and the depression of the 1930s seem to have had little effect on birds. There was perhaps a more scientific attitude prevalent among natural historians and it became less unusual to watch and take notes than to shoot and preserve specimens. Botanists, perhaps because they have so many more species to deal with, still maintain a large element of collecting in their studies, but in Britain, Europe and North America at least, the age of collecting was over by 1914. Julian Huxley showed the way with his detailed studies of the Great Crested Grebe's ritualized courtship displays. Others followed. David Lack's *Life of the Robin* was published in 1943, though based on field work carried out during the 1930s. As early as 1926 a young man called Hosking had decided to become Britain's first professional bird photographer: the fact that he didn't starve indicates that there must have been a market for his products. Bird books ceased to be records of the author's slaughters and became more concerned with documenting behaviour and distribution. Somewhat esoteric, middle-class societies such as the Royal Society for the Protection of Birds (RSPB) slowly expanded their membership, and a small group of field workers founded the British Trust for Ornithology (BTO). But it was the respite from continuous persecution, more by default than by any active means, that enabled the remnant populations of our scarcer birds to hold their own.

The effect of the Second World War, as far as the birds of these islands were concerned, was remarkably similar to that of the first. All the gamekeepers were 'drafted' and sent off to do battle, so once again birds of prey were allowed to flourish. Guns were at a premium and ammunition, even shotgun cartridges, far too valuable to waste on birds. This time, however, there was another fear — invasion. All possible landing places along the south and east coasts were heavily mined, wired and protected and, along the east coast in particular, areas of low-lying grazing were flooded to prevent the landings of German troops expected daily during the summer of 1940.

At Minsmere, an area of damp summer grazing was flooded, enabling over two miles of shoreline to be made safe from invasion from the nearby coast of Holland. Further north a similar scheme flooded the fields that lay between Dunwich and Walberswick, including the Walberswick football pitch on Corporation Marshes. The floods thus created were a natural home to marshland birds, waders and, as reeds grew up, herons and harriers. Suddenly there were new marshes where there had been none for over a hundred years. Birds that had become rare or even extinct as breeders could once again find homes along our shores, a process that culminated in the return of the Avocet after an absence of a hundred years.

While throughout both wars the vast majority of birds prospered, one species did not. Until 1914 Peregrines bred along much of our coastline, building their eyries on virtually every substantial headland. During the periods 1914–18 and 1939–45 a bounty was offered by the government on all Peregrines, due to their depreda-

Threatened by hunting, pesticides and war-time emergencies, the Peregrine survived them all. Now it faces persecution at the hands of falconers from the oil-rich Middle East.

tions on pigeons carrying urgent messages from the fighting front. The efficacy of 'pigeon post', even during the First World War, has been seriously questioned, and it seems quite ridiculous that important messages should have depended on such a means of transmission during the second war. Doubtless the idea seemed plausible to some Whitehall civil servant intent on contributing to the war effort from beneath his tin hat and gas mask, but one cannot help but feel that the Peregrine suffered in vain. To a nation equipped with radar, jamming devices, flight beams and sophisticated radio codes, the use of pigeons as message carriers is virtually medieval. Nevertheless, almost the entire Peregrine population of southern England was eliminated, amounting to about 600 birds, during the course of the hostilities. From a total population of about 650 pairs in 1939 its numbers were reduced to less than 500 pairs by 1947. It was, perhaps, the only British avian war casualty.

Once more, in 1945, the demobbed gamekeepers returned to their beats to carry on where they had left off in 1939. But now, more than ever, change was at hand. If fashions and attitudes had changed between 1914 and 1918, the changes that followed 1945 brought about a social and political revolution of far greater significance. Despite his personal magnetism and wartime leadership, Winston Churchill and the Conservative Party were rejected by the voters of 1945, who gave a Labour Party dedicated to change an overwhelming majority. The assault on traditional power and privilege that followed is easily overlooked, but the foundations (such as they are) of contemporary Britain were laid between 1945 and 1951. Most of these changes are of no concern to us here, but the overall and long-term effects on inherited wealth are still being felt. Slowly the great estates were broken up and passed into new and more vigorous hands. Shooting was less important to these new men than the efficiency and profitability of their land. Farm workers were less slavish than they had been before and the number of gamekeepers declined.

Then came the great Protection of Birds Act of 1954. Birds had been protected before, but on a piecemeal basis. The 1954 Act changed the emphasis of protecting by force of law: now it was no longer merely specific birds but all birds and their eggs that were protected. Basically the Act divided birds into three classes: those that were protected all the year round; those protected during a close season but which could be shot at other times — mainly sporting birds; and those — mainly pest species — which could be shot at all times. Additionally there were a number of exceptions designed to prevent the law looking an ass. These included allowing the taking of the eggs of a number of common birds that were otherwise protected so that every child who went birds' nesting did not automatically become a criminal, and preserving the right of the men of Ness to continue their traditional toll of the young Gannets on Sula Sgeir in the Outer Hebrides. The latter continues to the present day; the former was changed to protect even the eggs of common birds in 1967.

Thus, at a stroke, the pastimes of skin and egg collecting were made illegal and subject to penalties enforceable by law. Now, in addition to the rare vagrant, the majority of other birds could only be collected by special licence available on scientific grounds. Yet, like most laws, anomalies remained. Mounted specimens could still be bought and sold and are thus still to be seen in antique shops throughout the country. Birds' eggs, however, could not, and so the many extensive collections in private hands became worthless (legally at least) overnight. Strangely (or perhaps not), the Act put a virtual stop to the collection of skins, but did little to stop the activities of the hard-core eggers. Yet, like all legislation, it was only as good as the enforcement that backed it. Enforcement at that time depended on the local 'bobby' and magistrate, and the efforts of individuals and groups in bringing breaches of the law to the attention of the authorities. The work of the RSPB in this respect has been outstanding and it is to the Society's efforts that we owe the respect in which the 1954 Act was held, prior to its replacement by the Wildlife and Countryside Act of 1981.

These changes have had their effect on our birds. Today many species have as healthy a population as they have enjoyed for a hundred years. No doubt numbers of Kestrels, Sparrowhawks, Golden Eagles, Buzzards, harriers and owls are still killed every year by gamekeepers with the old attitudes. Many are killed by shotguns, though every year illegal pole traps are discovered in

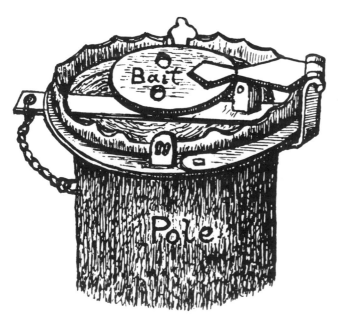

Pole traps were set up on top of a post in open countryside where they formed an ideal resting place for birds of prey. The technique is still practised illegally today.

some part of the country. Times are changing, however, and the old gamekeepers are being replaced by a younger generation of better-informed men with at least an elementary understanding of both the law and the relationships between predator and prey. Some species remain the gamekeeper's enemy.

The destruction wrought by a Tawny Owl on a flight cage of young Pheasants can be enormous, and even a modern, well-informed gamekeeper may decide to sit up with his shotgun and eliminate the menace. He does so, however, with the knowledge that he is breaking the law, not in ignorance of it. A fact which, in itself, is a great step forward. He knows also that it is the artificial situation of a super-abundance of food that has attracted the predator and that once dispersed his Pheasants will suffer only a normal (and tolerable) degree of predation. Thus his, admittedly illegal, killing is a response to a particular situation, not evidence of an all-out battle against predators. While it should be condemned, such predator control is at least understandable.

No better example of this newly-acquired tolerance toward predators can be found than the relationship between fish farmers and the Osprey. Increasing numbers of Ospreys now occur not only around their Scottish breeding haunts, but throughout the country. In spring their passage northward is swift and goes largely unnoticed. In autumn birds regularly stay off-passage for weeks at a time when they find a suitably rich feeding ground. While there are already some fishery managers calling for control of Ospreys on the grounds that their profit margins are being literally eaten by these great birds, most are not only tolerant but also feel privileged that an Osprey has favoured their ponds.

In today's terms a two-pound trout is worth about £3 and an Osprey may take one or two such fish every day. An immature bird, lacking the hunting skills of an adult, may grab and injure several fish before making a kill and thus cause considerable financial damage to what is fast becoming a highly competitive business. Yet the fishery owner will still recount with pride of the Osprey that spent a day or week with him last autumn. He knows that he is losing money, but also, via the media, that the Osprey is a decidedly rare bird in Britain and one that a great deal of time and money is being spent protecting. As a result there are few, if any, instances of Ospreys being shot by fish farmers, despite the obvious and direct economic connection.

It may be that our populations of birds injurious to the interests of gamekeepers are too small to worry about or to form a serious menace. But that, in itself, is a step forward, for it presupposes that gamekeepers can distinguish between the various species and have a background of knowledge that tells them which are harmless and which potentially destructive. Things are very different abroad.

Elsewhere in Europe the use of shotgun and poisoned egg is still very much everyday practice. Young game chicks, especially young Partridges, are particularly prone to harriers and the number of these birds to be seen on French or Spanish gamekeepers' gibbets has to be seen to be believed. Certainly a single gibbet may easily hold more Montagu's Harriers than the total British population, but that does not mean that we would have more birds were the slaughter to the south to stop. No doubt things will change for the better, but by then these birds may have been reduced to tiny numbers. At present the number of Montagu's Harriers quartering the plains of central Spain is still impressive — it is a pity that no-one has thought it worthwhile to investigate their prey during the critical period.

As far as bird legislation is concerned Europe is a mess; when it comes to enforcement the situation is chaotic. Birds may be protected on one side of a boundary and be legal quarry on the other. The chances are, however, that whatever the law it will not be enforced. The number of birds of prey shot in the cause of game protection in Europe every year must be enormous — yet it is doubtful if it increases the number of gamebirds by more than a small percentage.

Even in an enlightened country such as Britain several other birds are placed outside the law and liable to be destroyed at any time of the year. Jay, Magpie and Carrion Crow are the best examples and ones that even the most devout of conservationists would agree should be controlled. Many gamekeepers shoot them on sight throughout the year and their serried ranks are now the major avian decorations of the British gibbet. Yet there is no evidence that a century or more of constant persecution has seriously reduced their numbers. All three flourish and continue to take a toll of the eggs and chicks of a wide variety of other species — a fact which creates as many problems for those responsible for maintaining bird reserves as it does for the gamekeeper intent on keeping numbers of game species as high as possible.

At one time the idea of shooting birds within the confines of a nature reserve was quite unthinkable. Today it is recognized that the so-called 'balance of nature' is a myth. Nature is dynamic, always changing, and if we want to protect a certain species or type of bird then we must interfere with natural processes in much the same way as those whose object is the rearing of gamebirds. Of course, much of this work will involve the artificial creation and maintenance of suitable habitats. Left alone, marsh will quickly turn to scrub and ultimately to some type of forest, which is fine if woodland or scrub-dwelling birds are required. There is, however, no great shortage of woodland habitat in Britain, whereas there is a decided scarcity of marshland. So it is a simple choice between woodpeckers or Marsh Harriers. If Marsh Harriers are the choice then aquatic habitats must be artificially maintained — a system similar in kind to the artificial burning of heather moors to provide the maximum amount of Red Grouse habitat. But the similarities do not end there.

The gamekeeper and reserve warden may both maintain a policy of exterminating weasels, stoats and grey squirrels, all of which are major predators on birds, their eggs and young. They may both keep the numbers of Crows down to acceptable levels, though generally a population of these birds may be tolerated on a bird reserve. But is there very much difference between keeping Crows in check on a shoot and keeping gulls down on a bird reserve? Both have arisen as a direct result of creating an artificial situation by providing a surplus of prey. So the rearing of Partridges or Avocets, Pheasants or Godwits requires some direct interference with natural processes.

Alongside the legal changes there has been a remarkable change in the attitudes of the population in general towards birds and wildlife. From being at best apathetic towards birds, the general public has, over a period of no more than thirty years, become positively bird and nature orientated. So far has this change of attitude insinuated itself that words which were once the preserve of conservationists have been taken over by a variety of interests in recent years. The word 'environment' has been adopted by a ministry; 'habitat' has been picked up by a furniture store; and even 'conservation' itself has now come to be applied to all manner of preservation campaigns and organizations.

The origins of this changed attitude are, I believe, easily found — television and leisure. Television, invented in the 1930s, became freely available in the 1950s when the BBC started a regular daily service. Later ITV, and later still BBC2, provided a choice of programmes progressively more sophisticated in their presentation. One of the earliest nature programmes was 'Look'. Presented by a youthful Peter Scott it showed viewers the birds and other animals that share our countryside and introduced a new generation (some might say a new class) to wildlife. It was well received and, always keen to latch on to a winner, the mandarins of the BBC were quick to follow with more 'nature'. Armand and Michaela Dennis, complete with quaintly foreign accents and an endless succession of cuddly pets, took the armchair traveller through the wilds of the African plains and introduced him to wildlife on the grand scale. This same couple gave a first opportunity to a host of young professional wildlife cameramen, including Des and Jen Bartlett and Alan Root — perhaps the greatest exponents of the art working today.

Even more youthful than Peter Scott, an engaging enthusiast called David Attenborough took us on 'Zoo Quests' to far-off places, where he showed us some of the strangest animals and birds to be found on earth. With the coming of commercial television Aubrey Buxton of Anglia Television took up the challenge with his 'Survival' series that has continued to the present day.

I have not bothered to add up the total number of wildlife hours of television produced in a year — it is considerable. I believe that by bringing bird and other wildlife stories into our homes television producers have done more to conserve British birds than any other single factor. At first they showed, then they persuaded, now they educate and entertain. What was once the preserve of the galloping anthropomorphism of Walt Disney has been changed to such an extent that even ranking-conscious American television treats wildlife subjects comparatively seriously. They may have an attitude of 'all threat and menace without actual blood' but still the message gets through.

The social revolution that followed 1945 led not only to a more equitable redistribution of wealth, but also to legislation regarding the length of working day and week. The last thirty years have seen a reduction in the normal working week to five days and forty or less hours. Along with this free time has come a real (not just monetary) increase in wages and a prosperity that is beyond our grandfathers' dreams. By the 1970s not to have a motor car was unusual, and a surprisingly large percentage of car owners had put their newly-found freedom of travel to good use. The leisure business took off and sports such as sailing, canoeing, golf, fishing and a host of others boomed. People had the time, the money and the transportation to pursue their own interests and newly-acquired passions — many took to watching birds. From a homely little club of 15,000 members in the late 1950s the RSPB had grown to an organization of 340,000 plus members in 1980. Many, no doubt, are passively supporting a worthwhile cause, but a large percentage are keen naturalists.

Gradually, wearing a pair of binoculars became more associated with watching birds than going to the races. What were once lonely walks were becoming populated by hordes of figures clad in green parkas armed with glasses, telescopes and telephoto lenses. Clubs and societies grew, new groups were started, slide shows and films proliferated and businessmen responded. Fortunately (or unfortunately depending on one's standpoint) watching birds is a cheap hobby. A pair of binoculars and an identification guide are all that are required — given care both will last for years. Compare these meagre requirements with the gear that the average angler feels bound to lug around with him, with the money spent by even the dinghy sailor, or with the number of one-handed 'pairs' of Jack Nicklaus golf gloves. Nevertheless there were (and are) sufficient 'extras' to attract many into the wildlife business in one way or another.

Binocular manufacturers offer a splendid range of instruments, travel agents an ever-increasing array of tours. Hotels and airlines, having noticed that the main periods of bird interest lie outside their peak holiday periods, scurry round rustling up business. There are bird boxes, bird prints, bird table mats, bird feeders, even bird aprons, tea towels, shopping bags, stationery and napkins. But, above all, there are bird books — and this is another!

Admittedly, bird books are published by businessmen to make money; but they may nevertheless be useful tools to the bird-

A pair of Bewick's Swans winging over the marshes of East Anglia, where they winter in increasing numbers as a result of the benevolent conservation policy of recent years.

watcher and/or create an interest on the part of a potential beginner. There are so many bird books about that every child has probably been given one at one time or another. Most are good value (publishing is a highly competitive business) and today many are lavishly illustrated with wonderful colour photographs. Their influence may be larger than is generally realized.

Bird-watching is, then, a mass participation field sport and conservation a voice that cannot be ignored. Yet while anyone concerned with birds must welcome the ever-growing number of supporters to the cause, there is one major drawback in this situation. Turn loose a couple of hundred watchers in search of a rare breeding or wintering bird and, by disturbance, they will destroy the very thing they wish to see. It is not at all unusual for that many to descend upon a particular locality when the whereabouts of such a bird become known. Sadly the freedom to wander at will over many of the most rewarding bird spots has, of necessity, had to be curtailed. The new army of bird-watchers has provided the money to establish bird reserves, yet one of the first acts of reserve administrators is to restrict access. It is inevitable, but none the less saddening for all that. There was a time (and I am no geriatric) when it was possible to walk the walls along the Ouse Washes, meet no one, and put up flock after flock of duck and Bewick's Swans. Today these same Washes can be watched from wooden-built hides, one of which has central heating and double glazing. The wild swans virtually feed from the hand and many sport a garish array of multi-coloured rings.

On the Suffolk coast what was once a primitive six-seater hide overlooking a famous bird marsh is now a double decker with room for fifty or sixty, and inhabited, in summer at least, by children playing 'touch' and ladies with dogs and no binoculars. No doubt I am as guilty as anyone in publicizing the bird cause. I salute all new bird-watchers as adding to the ornitho-lobby — but my joy is tempered with a little sadness at the loss of a wilderness.

The point about this growing wealth of bird-watchers, and therein I include bird-photographers, bird-recordists and all the others, is that by sheer weight of number they have become something of a menace to the birds themselves. Some species have shown a remarkable degree of tolerance toward binocular toters, others cannot stand disturbance. Just how many watchers seek out the Norfolk Bean Geese in winter? How many sought the Honey Buzzards in that noted southern spot? We know that thousands view the Loch Garten Ospreys, but do we have to have that sort of over-organized paraphernalia wherever a rare bird occurs? Bird-watchers *en masse* may be the latest problem that our birds have to face, but there have been many much more serious threats between the 'brave new world' of the 1954 Act and the present.

To protect a bird adequately from direct persecution is important, but it is only part of the story. It is now illegal to shoot a Sparrowhawk or take its eggs. It is not illegal to fell the wood in which it nests. The Stone-curlew may be protected by special penalties under the law, yet there is no penalty for ploughing the sandy wasteland on which it breeds. Indeed such action may qualify for a government grant towards the costs involved. This habitat destruction may be far more damaging to a population of birds than any amount of direct destruction. Undoubtedly the greatest of all causes of bird destruction resulted from a change in agricultural techniques in the mid-1950s.

Ever keen to make a name for themselves, or profits for the company that employed them, or conceivably in an altruistic search for truth to the greater benefit of mankind, research chemists started playing with the structure of elements and started creating new ones. Some of these were found to have remarkable properties when it came to controlling insects, many of which were considered harmful both directly to man and to his crops and animals. The most famous and familiar of these substances is Dichlorodiphenyl-trichloroethane or DDT, as it is thankfully known for short. This was particularly valuable in preventing the spread of disease during the Second World War and afterwards was put to invaluable use in eradicating diseases like malaria from such areas as the *terai* jungles of Nepal.

Other substances followed and by the 1950s a group known jointly as the chlorinated hydrocarbons, which includes dieldrin, aldrin and heptachlor, was in widespread use as pesticides and seed dressings. That they were effective is undisputed. By eliminating insect attacks farmers were able to cut down their seed costs substantially and to increase the yield of an acre considerably. What was not known was that these new chemicals had a remarkably long life — that is, they were remarkably persistent.

About the mid-1950s ornithologists in many parts of the country began to notice more than the usual number of dead and dying birds. I well remember seeing a Carrion Crow struggling through the thick grass of a Hampshire plantation apparently completely out of control. All sorts of species were affected, though it was the larger and more obvious birds, such as the raptors and owls, that were most easily noted. Such mass deaths among wild birds are usually confined to a single species and are usually explained in terms of an epidemic disease. Mass deaths among such a large range of species could only mean poisoning. While corpses were reported by anyone with an eye to see, specialist workers studying birds of prey began to notice a dramatic fall-off in the rate of breeding success. Peregrines and Golden Eagles frequently failed to breed at all, and were sometimes noted eating their own eggs. Investigation revealed that the eggs of these species had significantly thinner shells than those collected during earlier periods and one could surmise that the adults had accidentally broken their eggs and cleaned up their nests by eating the mess. Additionally, fewer eggs were being laid and a lower percentage of these produced young. Clearly something was wrong here too.

Ornithologists, ever watchful of their status among the scientific establishment and regarding the study of birds (as they still do today) as at best an infant science and at worst a branch of traditional natural history, were cautious. The connection between the massive slaughter and aberrant behaviour of birds and the new agricultural chemicals was circumstantial, sufficient perhaps for a court of law but lacking the level of experimental exactitude demanded by a scientific discipline.

Similar phenomena had been reported elsewhere, notably in the United States, where the Peregrine population, for example, had been all but eliminated save for pollution-free Alaska. It fell to a naturalist-journalist, Rachael Carson, with her book *Silent Spring*, to spell out to a concerned public the desperate state that had been reached. In Britain, naturally, a committee was formed; but unlike so many such institutions this one had a definite sense of urgency. Led by Stanley Cramp, a master of the workings of such bodies, the link was forged and pressure brought to bear. The use of the dreaded chlorinated hydrocarbons as seed dressings was banned voluntarily. Soon bans were backed by the force of law and the use of these new compounds in agriculture was eliminated. The exact extent of the damage will never be known, but the affair came near to being the greatest of all wildlife disasters.

The difficulties involved in discerning a change in the population of an abundant bird are all too obvious. If the population of, say, Puffins on an island group drops from 'hundreds of thousands' to '125,000', who is to say that there has actually been a decline in the Puffin? Only recently have accurate counts of seabird populations been made: previously 'one, two, . . . lots' had been the prevalent attitude. But what is true of a countable population of seabirds is doubly true of a widespread and numerous small bird. If Spotted Flycatchers are absent from the garden this year, they may have just moved next door. On the other hand they may have declined. Or, conceivably, the previous year may have been an exceptional 'boom' year and things have simply returned to normal. The 'pesticides affair' brought home to ornithologists, and, indeed, to the government, the fact that our knowledge of the populations of British birds was quite inadequate. We had a good idea of the populations of Herons, Gannets and a few other comparatively scarce, or colonizing, species. We had some idea of the total number of other species, but it was based only on guesswork and some pretty unsophisticated maths. Certainly we did not have the techniques to determine a small percentage change in the numbers of a bird species that might act as an early warning of another disaster like that of the pesticides. Under the aegis of the BTO, the Common Bird Census (CBC) was established to sample and monitor our birds. The Common Bird Census is based on regular counts of singing male birds in a variety of habitats. Controlled by a strict code of rules, observers throughout the country are required to search areas varying in size around the two hundred acre mark. They are required to make a series of visits through the breeding season and to plot the position of each singing male on a map. The series of maps are then forwarded to the BTO, where trained interpreters are able to count the total population of the area to within a fine degree of exactness. The population of each species throughout the country is then totalled to form an index, using 1966 as a base year.

For the first time the birds of Britain could be accurately monitored, and comments like 'seems to be decreasing' or 'less than usual breeding' could be replaced by a scientifically-based index of the population. CBC workers will, I trust, forgive the sketchy nature of this thumbnail account, for what is important is the value of the census in providing the tool by which conservationists can at last warn of what is happening to our environment. The fineness with which even small declines can be picked out is of immense value and should ensure that any future disaster will be noted early enough to prompt immediate action.

A sudden drop in the number of Whitethroats passing through the bird observatory network in the spring of 1969 alerted the BTO to a disaster of unknown proportions. The Common Bird Census confirmed the disaster and within six months of the first hint of trouble the staff were busily seeking an explanation.

On this occasion there was little that could be done. The catastrophic drought in the Sahel zone immediately south of the Sahara had pushed the limits of the desert southwards by several hundred miles. The nomadic human inhabitants had suffered untold hardships and were starving by the thousand. Refugees from the drought were fleeing southwards as their traditional watering holes dried up one after another and seasonal grazing for their flocks and herds failed to materialize. The news filtered slowly through to the West and a massive aid campaign was launched. The BTO Common Bird Census indicated that Whitethroats had perished from the same cause, for the Sahel is their traditional wintering ground.

Both the pesticide fiasco and the Sahel drought episode show just how valuable the accurate study of bird populations is in indicating an environmental disaster. As with the miner's Canary (when it falls off its perch run like hell!), birds are an early warning of something wrong, a sort of 'ecological litmus paper' as one pundit described it. There can be little doubt that had the use of chlorinated hydrocarbons continued unabated, humans would have been the next to suffer.

These chemicals are, in the words of the scientist, highly persistent — that is they do not break down easily. They are absorbed by birds that feed directly on seeds and which may then die as a result. However, many such birds accumulate only a sub-lethal dose, which is then passed on to their predators. Thus it is the raptors that suffer most, as the chemicals in the bodies of their prey accumulate in their body fat. So it was the dramatic decline in the populations of birds of prey that did as much to avert a human disaster as anything. It is as powerful an argument for maintaining a healthy stock of these birds as any.

Once again it was the rarest of our birds that had suffered most. The populations of Peregrine and Sparrowhawk, species most dependent on other birds as prey, were decimated. The Sparrowhawk was quickly added to the protected list for, being both abundant and an enemy of game, it had previously been distinguished by being the only unprotected raptor in Britain. The fact

A female Sparrowhawk at the nest with its bright-eyed brood.
Once the only bird of prey not covered by law, its numbers were
reduced by pesticide poisoning and it is now a protected species.

that both species have today made a significant recovery is due to
the ban on chemicals in response to the work of a comparatively
small band of ornithologists and (I reluctantly admit) the work of
a committee!

No sooner, however, does one door close than another one slams
— to misuse an old cliché. By virtue of the prompt action in Britain
(elsewhere the persistent pesticides continued in use despite the
outcry by local naturalists) our population of raptors, though drastically reduced, was still viable. Soon a recovery could be discerned
and within a few brief years we enjoyed one of the healthiest populations of these birds in the Western world. As a result, falconers
throughout the world turned their attentions to our Peregrine

eyries in their search for young birds. The newly-found, oil-based, affluence of the Middle East increased the demand for falcons beyond the traditional areas of supply and the price of these birds rocketed. A brood of young Peregrines was soon worth several thousand pounds and eyrie after eyrie was illegally raided. Penalties prescribed by law were totally inadequate to deal with these newly-inflated rewards. Once again the Peregrine was under pressure. Estimates of the damage naturally vary, but perhaps as many as half of the known Peregrine eyries were robbed in 1979.

The way in which the law is flouted can be seen from a classic case of eyrie robbing in 1977. That summer Peter Byrne of Glasgow took a young Peregrine from a Scottish eyrie and lodged it in a garage at the home of Thomas Frame in Ayrshire. Meanwhile Norman Clephane of Kensington had persuaded Fergus MacPhail to advertise the bird on his college noticeboard and in the student newspaper, using his own name and telephone number. The advert was spotted and reported to the RSPB who sent along Stuart Housden, one of their special investigators, to contact MacPhail. He was offered the Peregrine for £1,000. Next time MacPhail was contacted the price had risen to £2,000, but the RSPB agent agreed to the price and a rendezvous was arranged. Clephane, who was apparently the ringleader, drove with the Peregrine and his cronies to London in a company car, breaking down en route and calling in the AA, who helped them on their way. RSPB agent Housden kept the appointment as arranged and the police arrested the gang as the bird was handed over. If it were not so serious, the amateurish attempts by four young men on the look out for some easy money would be funny. The point, however, is that there are similar gangs operating in Britain which perform flawless operations in a truly professional way. Clephane, MacPhail, Frame and Byrne were each fined £75 and ordered to pay £20 costs. If they had stolen jewellery or cash worth £2,000 they would have faced imprisonment.

Peregrines are great traditionalists, using the same site year after year, a fact which makes them particularly easy to raid. With but meagre resources available it is quite impossible for conservationists to mount a round-the-clock watch on every Peregrine eyrie in Britain. Laws can be updated, higher penalties can be imposed, but there would seem to be little that can be done to stop the rot. No doubt our population of these birds will decline, but as the number of Peregrines dwindles so will their price increase. It is a remarkable parallel to the nineteenth-century skin collector boom; the scarcer the bird becomes the greater the pressure on those that remain.

It would be nice to round of this survey of the recent history of British birds on a note of optimism, and it is true that many species are in a better state than they have been for years. Many birds that were exterminated in the past have returned to breed with us once more — their stories form the major part of this book. Others have recovered from some human-inflicted disaster only to face another even more serious one. It would not, I fear, be over-pessimistic to assume that other more insidious and as yet unknown disasters await our birds. I have said nothing about the persistent oil pollution that threatens our populations of seabirds. Nothing of the senseless slaughter of fish for fertilizer that has reduced the numbers of seabirds on the famous Guano Islands of Peru to a fraction of their former numbers. Nothing still of the continued explosion of the human population of the world with its attendant demands for food, power and other natural resources that year by year changes the face of the planet, and nothing of the destruction of forests on a worldwide scale, the increasing areas of desert, and of the virtually universal presence of DDT in the environment. Year by year species are exterminated while others are added to the danger list. Is it too pessimistic to look forward to the day when only those birds that can live alongside man will be left? Meanwhile the purpose of this book is to tell the story of conservation successes in the present century set against the background of the previous hundred years. If the reader finds cause for optimism in what follows I pray it will not prove to be a false optimism.

Chapter Four

Never to Return

While the senseless persecution that characterized a former age exterminated a number of British birds that have now, in these more enlightened times, made a comeback, there are some that have never returned. Yet, surprisingly enough, the list, depressing as it may be, is not a long one and is more than balanced by new birds that have bred with us for the first time. Those that have gone are mostly the large and spectacular, those that have taken their place small and obscure. Who, for instance, would be prepared to swop the Great Bustard for the Serin, the Spoonbill for the Collared Dove? Both of those desirable species have long since gone; only the White-tailed Eagle among this spectacular group has disappeared during the twentieth century.

Six species have been lost to Britain in historical times. Once, a million years ago or more, there were breeding albatrosses and pelicans, but they are pre-history as far as we are concerned; only their bones remain to tell us that they once existed within our shores. The history of British ornithology goes back, of course, to Roman times and beyond, though birds are mentioned only in passing and then mostly in relation to their culinary qualities. Nevertheless, actual records of birds do not really begin to appear until the seventh century, and the first bird books did not appear until much, much later.

By 700 AD Anglo-Saxon literature had recorded a list of fifteen species of British birds: Gannet, Whooper Swan, White-tailed Eagle, Crane, Quail, Whimbrel, Kittiwake, Carrion Crow, Raven, Cuckoo, Woodpigeon, Swallow, Nightingale, Robin and Chaffinch. Not, it must be pointed out, that only fifteen birds inhabited the country, nor even that bird-watchers of the Dark Ages could only recognize that number. Fifteen is simply the number of species actually recorded in the literature. Thereafter more writers added birds until by the time of Chaucer just under a hundred can be gleaned from the literature. Chaucer himself adds a further four to bring the list to a round hundred in 1382. A great leap forward took place when the first printed bird book *Avium Historia* by William Turner appeared in Latin in 1544. By 1600 about 150 species had been recognized and recorded in Britain and it is at this point that most histories of British birds begin.

The Crane bred until the sixteenth century and may well have lingered on past 1600. It is first mentioned by Ethelbert II, King of Kent until 760 AD, in a letter requesting a falcon suitable to fly at the local Cranes. Much later King John flew Gyrfalcons at Cranes in Cambridgeshire in December 1212 AD, with considerable success, and in the reign of Edward IV no less than 204 Cranes were served at the banquet to celebrate the enthronement of Archbishop Neville. Certainly such feasts could hardly rely on imported birds and, equally certainly, the Crane population of the time must have already been under considerable pressure. A young 'Pyper Crane' was obtained by 'Notyngham of Hyklyng' in 1543 and it is on this

Long since gone as a British breeder, the Crane is now only the most erratic of visitors and is unlikely to settle with us and trumpet over the marshes in display.

record that the breeding of the Crane in Norfolk (Hyklyng = Hickling Broad) is based. It is also the last positive evidence of the species' breeding with us. So the Crane was, perhaps, the first British bird to be lost in historical times: it remains today a rather scarce passage migrant in spring and autumn, with the occasional large influx when Scandinavian birds lose their way between their breeding grounds and their winter quarters in Spain.

The next bird to go was the Spoonbill, which certainly bred in England well into the seventeenth century. Sir Thomas Browne

Once a breeding bird of the Fen district of East Anglia and of Bishop's Park in Fulham, the Spoonbill may soon return to the coastal marshes of eastern England where it lingers each spring.

mentions breeding at Reedham in Norfolk and Trimley in Suffolk about 1668. 'The Shovelard . . .' he writes '. . . now [breed] at Trimley . . . . They come in March and are shot by fowlers, not for their meat, but for the handsomeness of same.' These were the last records. Previously the Spoonbill had nested at Weestewood and Haselette near Goodwood in Sussex in 1570 and in Pembrokeshire in 1602. In 1523 the Bishop of London sued one of his tenants for breaking into Bishop's Park in Fulham to take herons and 'Shovelers' (as Spoonbills were then called) that were nesting in the trees. This Park still exists in Fulham on the north side of Putney Bridge, but sadly Spoonbills are hardly likely to return to such a scanty patch of green in London's urban sprawl. These birds, too, were a favourite at banquets and Henry VIII certainly ate them in 1531.

Next, in chronological order, was the Great Auk, which bred on St Kilda, probably also on Papa Westray in Orkney, and conceivably on the Isle of Man and on Lundy. Great Auks were killed for meat, for feathers, for their fat for fuel and for macabre amusement. By 1800 only a very few of these birds remained and almost all records refer to birds killed. The last North American Great Auks were taken in 1819 on Funk Island off Newfoundland, where in 1534 they were said to be abundant. The last British bird was caught by L. M'Kinnon and D. MacQueen on Stac an Armin on St Kilda in 1840. They kept it alive for three days but then blamed the occurrence of a storm on the bird and killed it as a witch. But the loss of the last British Great Auk was also more or less the extermination of the species as a whole, for on 4 June 1844 three Icelandic fishermen discovered and killed the last known pair and smashed their egg into the bargain. The Great Auk will never come back to breed in Britain, nor anywhere else.

About the same time as the Great Auk was being exterminated for all time in the north, the Great Bustard was being shot out of existence away to the south in its last British haunts. Though this bird was probably never widespread, and indeed possibly not present prior to 1460, the enclosures of the former common land

The Great Auk is the one bird that ceased to breed with us in historical times and which we can be quite certain will never return: it was exterminated in the last century.

and open fields, together with the subsequent hedging and planting of windbreaks, destroyed the Bustard's habitat. Earlier it had been served at medieval banquets, and it was taken by greyhounds on Newmarket Heath. But it would be erroneous to think of the Great Bustard as ever having been a numerous species. Doubtless, too, it had always been an expensive bird, for as early as the sixteenth century it fetched ten shillings and during the reign of Henry VIII the Bustard was protected by law. Anyone found guilty was, according to the Act, upon pain of imprisonment for one yeare, and to lose and forfeit for every egge of any Bustarde so taken or distroid 20 pence, the one moitie thereof to be to the King our Soveraigne Lorde, and the other halfe to him that will sue for the same in forme aforesaide.

By 1775 it was quite definitely becoming scarce and a law of George III protected the species during the breeding season. No doubt Bustards were difficult to shoot with a crossbow, but the advent of the gun changed all that. In his *Rural Sports* Daniel notes that Mr Crouch of Burford had shot a Hen Bustard at forty yards with a fowling piece, using partridge shot, in 1800. Yet by then the Bustard was in a poor way and about to disappear from its stronghold on Salisbury Plain.

In 1811 a horse rider caught a male Bustard high on the downs near Tilshead and presented it to his host Mr J. Bartley, who insisted on giving him a small reward. Kept alive on a diet of mice and sparrows the Bustard was soon after sold to Lord Temple for a princely thirty guineas. The following year the Salisbury area held a flock of seven, and individuals may have lingered until 1820. While obviously regretting the demise of the Wiltshire Bustards the Reverend Alfred Smith, to whose account I am greatly indebted, also notes:

> When I was in Portugal in the spring of 1868, I was so fortunate as to procure a magnificent male (Great Bustard) . . . in the flesh . . . whose body, after I had taken off the skin, for several days formed a large item in the bill of fare of the Hotel Braganza at Lisbon . . .

Such 'good fortune' abroad only parallels the 'good fortune' of others in the Reverend Smith's native land. Meanwhile in Norfolk in 1812, the head gamekeeper at Wretham, one George Turner, had perfected his own method of exterminating Great Bustards. By systematic baiting with food he encouraged quite decent-sized flocks within range of a battery of four large guns, where up to seven birds were killed at a time.

By 1826 the Great Bustard had disappeared from the Yorkshire Wolds as it had already gone from Lincolnshire, Hampshire, Sussex, Cambridgeshire, Hertfordshire and Berkshire, in all of which it had previously bred. In 1819 there were but two droves left in the country; one north of Swaffham and Westacre in Norfolk,

where twenty to thirty could still be found; the other around Thet-
ford and Icklingham in Suffolk, where up to forty could be seen.
From this date onwards numbers declined fast. The last breeding
was reported from Elveden in 1832 when a female was seen with a
single chick in July by Hoy and Salmon. Though a law was passed
in 1831 protecting the Bustard from 1 March to 1 September it was
already too late. By 1833 only the Norfolk drove at Swaffham
remained and all were apparently females. Eggs were laid most
years, but failed to hatch. Some birds lingered until 1838, and
possibly to 1843 or 1845: thereafter the English Great Bustard
disappeared. From that time onwards it was an irregular visitor,
with some winters bringing a considerable influx as in 1870–1,
1879–80 and 1890–1. Single birds occurred from time to time, but
since the First World War they have been decidely rare and highly
irregular in their appearances here. Only seven were reported in the
twenty years between 1958 and 1978, though the last, at St
Nicholas-at-Wade in Kent, was a male that stayed from 7 January
to 8 April, to the delight of hundreds of bird-watchers.

As it seemed highly unlikely that the Great Bustard would ever
recolonize Britain of its own accord, an attempt was begun in the
early 1970s to reintroduce the bird on Salisbury Plain. Lest such
action should lead to immediate criticism it should be mentioned
here that there are several birds that now breed quite freely in
Britain following deliberate and accidental introductions. Notable
among this group are Little Owl and Canada Goose. It is also easily
overlooked that our present population of the Capercaillie is
descended from Scandinavian stock introduced at Kenmore by
Loch Tay following the extermination of our native birds. And
finally that it is the Nature Conservancy Council itself that is
attempting to reintroduce the White-tailed Eagle in Scotland.

The idea of attempting to bring the Great Bustard back to Britain
was the brain-child of the Hon Aylmer Tryon, who founded the
Great Bustard Trust in 1970. Mr Tryon, who runs the wildlife
Tryon Gallery in London's Dover Street, is a well-known Wiltshire
naturalist. The Trust arranged with the Ministry of Defence to lease
four hectares of their remote Porton Down site in the Wiltshire
chalklands, and erected a fox-proof fence to enclose the birds. A
stock of young, unfledged, Portuguese birds was imported and
quarantined at a private bird collection before being pinioned and
released at the Down.

A male Great Bustard displaying to an attentive group of hens. This huge bird could not stand the pace of change and, despite an attempted reintroduction, seems unlikely to return.

At this point the ideas of the Trust differed considerably from those of Bustard-rearing schemes in other parts of Europe. Quite deliberately the birds were visited as infrequently as possible. Food was put out in trays for them by a local farmer, but otherwise they lived a 'wild' life inside their enclosure and soon lost the trust of man that had developed during their period in quarantine. The idea behind this policy was simple — the captive birds would be wary and wild, would breed within the confines of the fox-proof enclosure, and then the young would fly free over the surrounding downland and establish a feral population.

However, it was soon realized that there were several disadvantages to this procedure. The enclosure was sufficiently large for birds to disappear for days at a time, arousing fears for their safety. Also, if a bird did die the opportunity to perform a post-mortem while the corpse was fresh would be easily lost. Injured birds would be difficult to locate and catch, and, above all, the finding and watching over nests, the object of the whole exercise after all, would prove exceptionally difficult.

In addition, it was soon discovered that the natural vegetation of the area, which had not been ploughed for at least a century, was quite unsuitable, providing neither sufficient cover nor food for the birds. Experiments with various crops and a system of sub-enclosures was tried, including the use of a dividing fence to separate the sexes after the disastrous 1978 season during which the four adult males failed to display. Pinioned birds are generally recognized as being less fertile, but these uninterested males were preventing the females from feeding, and they, as a result, were developing a stiffness of the leg joints that had already killed two of their number.

The separation of the sexes had three advantages: it enabled the females to be fed properly and gain full breeding condition; it enabled a more natural grouping into single-sex flocks outside the breeding season; and it also facilitated the administration of the hormone methyltestosterone to the males without fear of the females taking it accidently in their food.

By spring 1979 the Trust had four males and four females, all mature, including one female that had arrived as a vagrant at Fair Isle. For eight years the Bustards had lived happily enough but without sign of courtship, display or even making a scrape. The situation was desperate and called for desperate measures. Male hormone was added to the food of the males, while one male, who had always been tame and easy to catch, was given an implant of testosterone under the skin of the neck, a procedure that would allow a gradual release of hormone into the body over a period of sixty days.

Despite various difficulties — including one male jumping the barrier and prematurely joining the females, and the problem of administering the hormone in food and ensuring that both the remaining males were adequately dosed, while he of the implant was not overdosed — the birds were reunited on 8 April. Within a week the implanted male was displaying vigorously and continued to do so until June. Another male produced a full display, but only on five observed occasions. No mating was seen.

On 10 June Aylmer Tryon was watching over two hens presumed to be sitting on nests in a central reservation out of bounds to the males. Until this moment no one had entered to check the possible nesting, in an effort to keep disturbance to an absolute minimum. When one bird left her presumed nest to feed, a Rook immediately dashed in and started hacking at the site. Mr

Tryon and his companion, local aviculturalist F.K. Bromley, promptly rushed in causing panic to Rook and Bustards alike. Where the Rook had landed was a nest with two eggs, one with a large hole. The second nest contained only eggshell fragments.

In view of the disturbance it was decided that the female Bustard would be unlikely to continue incubating and both eggs were removed to Mr Bromley's incubator. The damaged egg was clearly fertile, but it was removed after one night when the yolk began bubbling from beneath the artificial seal. The second egg was incubated and later placed under a broody hen. Unfortunately it was rejected and, in the process, cracked. It was sealed, returned to the incubator, and eventually began hatching on 28 June. After being helped from the shell, dried, fed on house crickets and warmed, the chick began to weaken on 1 July and died the following night. So the first British-born Great Bustard for over a hundred years had perished after only a few days. Lessons had been learned, however, and everyone was hopeful of a more successful outcome in 1980.

Dr N.J. Collar recalls that season:

> The tame male Arthur was once again given a testosterone implant at the start of February, and the whole sequence followed thereafter very much as in 1979. Two females laid (the 'Fair Isle hen' died almost exactly ten years after she was caught in the early spring) and eggs from one of these nests were taken in for artificial incubation while the other clutch was left. The three artificially incubated eggs all hatched, but only the first of them appeared to have sufficient strength to survive. The other two sadly died within a few days of hatching and, even worse, the healthy chick contrived to choke on a small particle of regurgitated food, about which nobody could do a thing (it was only at the post mortem that it was discovered why the chick should suddenly have had a seizure). As a final blow, the nest left for natural rearing was inexplicably deserted, and only a single egg was found at the nest scrape; whether other eggs had been laid is unknown.

So another season, during which hopes had been high for success, came to nothing. Dr Collar summarizes the situation thus:

> It seems ironic in the extreme to announce that this abysmal year should make the Trust the second most successful Great Bustard captive breeding scheme ever; but the fact is that no one has ever got the species to hatch eggs two years in succession other than the great Wolfgang

Gewalt when he kept the birds at Berlin Zoo. Now, however, the Trust is in obvious difficulties, having four males, but only three females. Unless some new females are found very quickly, the experiment will clearly founder. I think . . . this would be a particular pity at this stage, just when the chance is arising to test whether or not reintroduction really could work.

To see a White-tailed Eagle soar along the cliffs of some remote Scottish headland is not a privilege that has been granted to many alive today. After two centuries of ruthless persecution the last birds built their eyrie in Skye in 1916. Thereafter it became extinct as a breeding bird and was noted only as a very rare vagrant until 1968.

The history of the Sea Eagle, as it is often called in Britain, is a well-documented account of senseless destruction. At one time this was a quite common bird and there may have been more pairs of this than of the Golden Eagle, though Leslie Brown doubts this. Yet, despite its depredations on Red Grouse, the latter survived while the Sea Eagle was exterminated. Writing as late as 1871 Robert Gray says 'Being a much commoner bird [than the Golden Eagle] . . . the Sea Eagle has never been at any time in the same danger of extinction.' How mistaken he was.

At one time the White-tailed Eagle bred from Iceland right across northern and eastern Europe to Siberia and the Pacific at Kamchatka. It may still be numerous over parts of this vast range, but persecution has certainly eliminated it from huge areas. Even in India, where birds are generally ignored, it has declined as a winter visitor from its central Siberian breeding quarters, while in Europe it has become progressively rare. Today its western headquarters are in Norway, where among the myriad of coastal islands it finds a secure stronghold and may number as many as five hundred pairs. Yet even here, the birds had a price on their heads until comparatively recently and many were shot as a result.

By the end of the nineteenth century the White-tailed Eagle (it is frequently called the Erne in contemporary literature) was virtually extinct on the Scottish mainland. In a masterly piece of research documented in *The Birds of Scotland* the Misses Baxter and Rintoul outline the decline county by county. In the southern hills it certainly bred until the mid-nineteenth century. At Cairnsmore it was evidently still just surviving in 1852, though it continued to breed until at least 1866. In Ayrshire a traditional Eagle eyrie at Straiton was raided in 1812, and the bird continued to breed until 1840. A little earlier it had disappeared from the cliffs of Manor in Peebles-shire where it had long been resident. In Perthshire it ceased to breed prior to 1870 when the birds of Loch na Baa were poisoned, though it had formerly been quite common on Rannoch Moor. In Aberdeenshire it had nested among the seabirds at Troup and Pen-nan Heads, and in a pine on an island in Loch Loyne that was felled in 1835, after which the birds took to nesting in birches. In Argyll, where they continued breeding much later, the story of destruction is better documented. That noted egg collector John Wolley records (with Alfred Newton in their *Ootheca Wolleyana* 1864–1907) an egg taken in the county in 1853, and there are other records of eggs collected until 1876. In Ross-shire the birds nested until 1889 in Beinn Damph Forest. Further north still, in Suther-land, John Wolley was busily collecting their eggs in 1849 and described them as 'abundant'. As late as 1866 Harvie-Brown stated that they were 'still not uncommon' and in 1879 a well-established eyrie on the magnificent cliffs of Clo Mor was raided by John Colquhoun who shot one of the adults. Thereafter the survivor remained mateless. An eyrie at Handa, now an RSPB reserve, was deserted by 1864 and the story of continuous egg collecting of these Sutherland White-tailed Eagles continues through the 1870s and 1880s into the twentieth century. The noted collector F.C. Jour-dain, in whose honour an oological society was formed, procured a clutch in 1901.

On the Scottish islands the bird continued its rearguard action. But from eyrie after eyrie the story is the same — birds slaughtered and eggs collected. It had deserted Ailsa Craig early in the nineteenth century, but still bred on Arran in 1849 and may have done so again before the last known nest was deserted in 1870. On Islay it bred into the twentieth century, but three well-established sites on Eigg were deserted by 1877. On Rhum (more of which anon) the White-tailed Eagle was common enough for a man to kill five in a single day in 1825. Even in 1866 a gamekeeper killed eight in the year, and they were still present in 1892. Despite such depredations they struggled into the twentieth century, but last nested about 1907. An established pair on Canna survived until their eggs were taken in 1875.

In 1871 Robert Gray noted that the Isle of Skye was then the species' headquarters. 'Nearly all the bold headlands of Skye are frequented by at least one pair of Sea Eagles.' H.A. Macpherson noted in 1886 that formerly up to forty Eagles might be seen together at one time, and records the abandonment, one by one, of the coastal and offshore eyries. By 1889 they were virtually gone and the last authenticated White-tailed Eagles of Britain bred on Skye in 1916.

In the Outer islands the birds hung on in good numbers until the mid-nineteenth century, and Harvie-Brown noted that there seemed to have been no decline between 1888 and 1902. Yet from many a traditional eyrie there are records of eggs collected and breeding abandoned. In 1836 a Lewis man destroyed thirteen Eagles for a reward of five shillings each. Yet by 1902 Harvie-Brown was assured that the shepherds in the same area had specific instructions not to molest these birds. It did little to stem the tide that was running against the White-tailed Eagle in the Outer Hebrides. Exactly when it ceased to breed remains a mystery. Harvie-Brown's comments about 1902 'scarcely any diminution since 1888 [on Harris]' and 'no molesting in Park Deer Forest' are not supported by documentation of breeding. The last known breeding spot was his own record on the Shiant Islands in 1887.

In Orkney the story is the same. By 1841 the White-tailed Eagle was decidedly scarce, though eggs were taken year after year until 1877, and birds were still seen near traditional eyries until 1882. Shetland, however, was always more productive and there are records of Eagles breeding into the present century. Clutches of eggs were taken frequently from traditional eyries as late as 1900 and 1901, and in 1904 an egger was caught robbing an eyrie at Graveland on Yell and was apparently punished. By 1899 only five pairs were known; by 1908 only a single pair on Unst remained. The male was then shot and his albino mate was left to live in solitary existence as the last Shetland White-tailed Eagle until she disappeared in 1918. In Ireland it bred on the cliffs of Munster, Connaught and Ulster until the middle of the nineteenth century, but the last eyrie was found in 1898. In England it bred on Culver Cliffs on the Isle of Wight until 1780, the Isle of Man until 1815 and previously in the Lake District and Devon.

The destruction of the White-tailed Eagle in Britain was a direct result of human persecution. There is no question of habitat destruction, accidental poisoning by pesticides, of a changing climate affecting its distribution, or of any cause other than human persecution. Throughout their range these powerful birds are primarily scavengers and in Scotland there is no doubt that they frequently fed on the corpses of dead lambs. There also seems little doubt that they also occasionally killed live young lambs, so it is perhaps not surprising that shepherds took every opportunity they could to destroy the birds, though where there is a plentiful supply of seabirds, the Eagles seldom take sheep. Rewards for their slaughter were paid in many parts of the country, including ten shillings a head in Skye — a not inconsiderable amount at the time. Shooting and trapping were both highly effective, particularly of a bird that generally did not choose to build its eyries in remote and inaccessible areas. In 1888 one writer noted, 'I have seen the heads and feet of this bird nailed in dozens to the kennel doors, in company with one or two of those of the Golden Eagle, and numbers of Ravens, Buzzards and Peregrines.' By the latter part of the nineteenth century its numbers were so small that it merited a special place in the hearts (and cases) of the collectors. Birds were shot off the nest and their eggs taken on a considerable scale, aided no doubt by the freedom with which their whereabouts would be given by shepherds intent on their destruction.

Fifty years after the last White-tailed Eagle had disappeared from Britain the first attempt to reintroduce the species was attempted at Fair Isle. Introductions, even reintroductions of birds that have become locally extinct by human agency, are the subject of hot debate among ornithologists. Certainly much havoc has been caused around the world by introducing foreign and stronger elements into a delicate ecosystem without due thought and consideration. The destruction of so much of the ecologically-isolated avifauna of New Zealand is a classic case in point. Yet while there was always a chance that the highly migratory Osprey would recolonize Britain quite naturally, the White-tailed Eagle population of Norway is virtually resident and the likelihood of recolonization infinitesimal. For the same reason introduced Eagles are more likely to stay put than many other species. So in 1968

The White-tailed Eagle, seen here with young, was forced into extinction early in this century. Despite a substantial reintroduction programme, we still await news of it breeding with us again.

George Waterston of Scotland and J.F. Willgohs of Norway arranged for the release of four young Eagles on Fair Isle, in an attempt to persuade them to settle and breed. As it turned out this was not the ideal choice of locality, for records of this bird on the island were restricted to a report by the inhabitants in 1862 that it used to breed and the presence on the map of an 'Erne's Hill'. But it is easy to be wise after the event. One of the four eaglets was killed by having its plumage coated with the oil ejected by young Fulmars on which it attempted to prey. There were no Fulmars on Fair Isle prior to 1903 and indeed the spectacular spread of this bird around our coasts did not really get under way much before the White-tailed Eagle was already extinct. The remaining three eaglets disappeared over the next fourteen months. Clearly Fair Isle was not the right site.

In 1975 the Nature Conservancy Council started a second reintroduction scheme, this time based on the Isle of Rhum in the Inner Hebrides where the Eagle had last bred in 1907. Four eaglets were imported from Norway and, though the male died, three females were reared and released. This process was repeated in subsequent years until, by the autumn of 1979, fourteen males and fifteen females had been released. Three others, imported in 1976 and 1977, were kept tethered to provide a potential captive breeding stock as a back-up to the released population. But in 1979 these too were released. One soon died, but the older pair survived and settled. To date three other birds have been found dead within two months of their release.

The rate of survival seems to be high and birds have learned to feed at special food dumps established for their benefit, where a varied menu of fish, gulls and venison offal is provided. The young birds take advantage of natural carrion and also quickly learn to kill seabirds. Sometimes the eagles form flocks and up to six have been noted together at a Rhum food dump. There is even some evidence that established birds will take the new season's releases 'into care' and virtually 'adopt' them during the critical few months after release. Nevertheless there is a certain amount of wandering and birds have been reported from as far away as Northern Ireland, Islay and Inverness.

By the end of 1979 there had been frequent displays of talon-gripping and tumbling, but no evidence of breeding. As these birds take five years to reach maturity, results, in the form of wild breeding, cannot be expected until at least the early 1980s. Meanwhile a continued supply of young birds from Norway would seem to be required simply to maintain numbers and the age balance of the population. Perhaps one day these magnificent birds of prey will once more be seen soaring around our seabird cliffs, but to expect them ever to re-establish themselves in their former numbers, estimated by Leslie Brown at around two hundred pairs, would seem to be immensely optimistic. Though two eaglets are commonly reared, the average is 1.6 young per nest in Norway and 1.4 in Iceland; so it would still be a long long time before a healthy population could be established in Scotland.

*　　　*　　　*

Of the handful of species that have disappeared since the history of British birds began in about 1600, the White-tailed Eagle may well return with the aid of man. It could be joined by the Great Bustard, which may have been introduced in the first place. Thus by the year 2000 AD we could have healthy populations of both species, and have lost only the Crane, Spoonbill and Great Auk; and who is so bold as to predict the future breeding, or otherwise, of the Spoonbill in this country? The Great Auk has gone, the Crane is unlikely to colonize — for four centuries of destruction it is really not such a bad score.

Chapter Five

Back from the Brink

The extermination of the Great Auk, the Great Bustard and the White-tailed Eagle was but the tip of an iceberg of destruction that seriously affected virtually every large British bird. Only good fortune prevented several other species from following the same path, perhaps never to return. Birds of prey were particularly prone to destruction in the later half of the nineteenth century as gamekeepers sought to eliminate them as vermin, skin and egg collectors sought them because of their increasing rarity, and Victorian homes sought them as be-domed decorations. It is only a matter of luck that the Red Kite did not disappear and it is the story of this once common bird that best epitomizes the slaughter and destruction meted out by our Victorian forebears.

The Red Kite was, in the early eighteenth century, both common and widespread, being found in conspicuous numbers over the streets of London, occupying the same niche as the Black Kite in Cairo and the Pariah Kite in Delhi. Yet these latter birds are often regarded as conspecific and it has been the subject of some debate among ornithologists as to the exact identity of these London Kites. But the fact remains that the Red Kite was at one time plentiful in many parts of Britain. Yet by 1870 it was extinct in England, by 1900 extinct in Scotland, and at about the same time was reduced to a handful of birds in central Wales.

In former times travellers from the Continent were quick to remark on the number of Kites that frequented the streets of London whereas, as is so often the way, the locals took them for granted. Thus in 1465 Baron Leo van Rozmital, the King of Bohemia's brother-in-law, wrote

---

1	*1. Wings spread over the shores of Britain for the first time in fifty years, the White-tailed Eagle was reintroduced to the Isle of Rhum in the 1970s.*
2	*2. Taking advantage of the opportunities offered by the war-time respite in hunting, the Avocet was a natural recolonist to the flooded coastline of Suffolk and has flourished ever since.*

Nowhere have I seen so many Kites as on London Bridge. It is a capital offence to kill them. The Londoners say they keep the streets of the town free from all filth. They are so tame that they often take out of the hands of little children the bread smeared with butter in the Flemish fashion, given to them by their mothers.

Shakespeare referred to London as 'city of Crows and Kites', while in 1555 Belon declared that Kites were hardly less common in London than in Cairo. Certainly it was a protected species in the city at that time, along with the Raven. No doubt it was less common in the countryside because of the lack of garbage and carrion, but it frequently raided the chickens that wandered at will in village and farmyard, and was doubtless greeted with less than enthusiasm by the population. It was in the countryside that the Glead (or Glider) as it was known had a price on its head, even in those days. The churchwardens of Tenterden in Kent recorded

1676 — ffrancis Peck, for 3 dozen and a halfe of Kyte's heads and one hedghogg's head, one shilling and a penny. 1680 — Wm. Baker for 16 crowe's heads, one hedghogg's head, 2 Kyte's heads and 5 Raven's heads, one shilling and threepence. 1683 Tho. Curteis for 4 Kytes and 1 Sparrowhawke, tenpence.

In twelve years no less than 428 Kites were paid for, an average of thirty-six a year in this small Kentish parish. It still bred in the trees at St Giles-in-the-Fields in 1734, and in 1777, having noted that it still nested in Gray's Inn, Pennant sent young to Gilbert White. It was perhaps extinct by the end of the century and is now only the rarest of rare vagrants. A correspondent told me of one seen over Lords in the 1960s, during a particularly dull day of cricket.

The establishment of hunting at the beginning of the nineteenth century and the protection of game preserves by gamekeepers had a sudden and quite profound effect on the Kite. As James Fisher has pointed out

early persecution, directed against the Kite as a chicken stealer, was in

Opposite. *After a century of persecution the Red Kite found its last stronghold in the mountains of central Wales, where an enlightened conservation policy has enabled it to thrive once more.*

the breeding season. Most of the heads paid for by the churchwardens
... all over England were ... of young taken from the nest. ... The
gamekeeper, armed with new and more effective weapons, exterminated the Kite ... from the records of half the counties of England
at the beginning of the nineteenth century.

As Robert Smith noted in his *Universal Directory for Destroying
Rats and other Kinds of Four-footed and Winged Vermin*, 1768,
there was a bounty on the heads of Kites. From county after county
they disappeared: Kent, 1815; Berkshire, Oxfordshire, Cambridgeshire, Norfolk, Suffolk and Northumberland, 1830; Huntingdonshire, 1837; Cumberland and Rutland, 1840; Northamptonshire,
1845; Worcestershire, 1850; Essex, 1855; Lincolnshire, 1870 — the
last English Kites. The story is paralleled in Scotland.

In 1871 Gray noted 'From being a very common bird in many of
the wooded districts of Scotland, the Kite, or Salmon-tailed Gled,
as it is called, has become almost as scarce as the Goshawk or
Osprey.' Though always (and not surprisingly) rare in the Outer
Isles and northernmost Scotland, and decidedly local among the
Border Hills, elsewhere the Kite was common enough during the
eighteenth century. Then came the shotgun and the most extraor-
dinarily speedy extermination campaign. Just in time E.T. Booth,
of Dyke Road Museum fame, secured two youngsters from Glen
Lyon in Perthshire in 1876. Three years later he was back in Scotland again to complete his collection, which already included a
female, eggs and the young of 1876, with a male. 'I could plainly see
his shadow thrown through the upper branches of the trees before
he came into view; and as there was some open space round the nest,
he afforded the easiest possible shot, and fell dead as a stone at my
feet.' Booth then took a youngster from the nest and reared it till
it reached the size and plumage he required before killing it as a
specimen. Together with John Colquhoun and the notorious Englishman Charles St John, Booth was responsible for the extermination of the last Scottish Kites.

Until 1879 the fishing tackle suppliers, Andersons, had a regular
supply of a couple of Kites a year from Perthshire for feathers for
tying flies. Drummond Hay noted breeding in 1880, though he was
not to know that his record constituted one of the last Scottish nests
of the species. There are records from Rothiemurchus about the

same time, from Ross-shire in 1883 and Caithness in 1884. Thereafter we have only reports of individuals, save for a note from
Mathieson that a pair nested in Glen Garry in 1917. The First World
War, and the respite from persecution that it offered to birds in
general and birds of prey in particular, was just forty years too late
for the Scottish Kites.

As Baxter and Rintoul note in *The Birds of Scotland*: 'The prin-
cipal feature of the disappearance of the Kites in Scotland was the
rapidity with which it was effected.' In a single season in 1824–5,
in the Callander Hills, 105 Kites were killed. In Glengarry, in the
three years 1837 to 1840, no less than 275 succumbed, though the
chances of misidentification were doubtless high. Similar examples
are far from rare in the literature and it is clear that no species could
survive such an all-out war of attrition.

By 1905 there were between nine and twelve Kites left in an area
referred to as 'central Wales', but which we now know to have been
in the upper Towy valley above Llandovery. Elsewhere in Europe
the situation was remarkably similar. In Sweden a healthy population was decimated and by the time protection was provided in
1914, there were no more than fifty pairs breeding in the southern-
most provinces. In Denmark the Kite was common until the middle
of the nineteenth century, but was then decimated and ceased to
breed after 1920. In Germany it was already scarce by the middle
of the nineteenth century, and decidedly rare by the turn of the
century. Its numbers increased during or following the Second
World War, but thereafter declined once more. As could be expected, it was the lack of firearms in the late 1940s that enabled the Kite
population to expand. France, too, slaughtered its Kites during the
nineteenth century, and the decline continues today. The story is
paralleled in Italy, Spain, Austria, Poland and so on throughout
Europe.

The Welsh Kites, balanced on a knife-edge, were still persecuted
ruthlessly by egg collectors well aware of the extremely low ebb
that the population had reached. The situation was also recognized
by J.H. Salter, Professor of Botany at Aberystwyth, who had seen
virtually every nest between 1893 and 1903 robbed, and the
occasional adult shot by collectors. On 13 February 1903 Salter
wrote to the British Ornithologists' Club in an effort to gain their
support for the protection of the Welsh Kites. The result was the

establishment of the Kite Committee consisting of J.L. Bonhote, W.E. de Winton, E.G.B. Meade-Waldo, the Hon. W. Rothschild, Howard Saunders and Watkin Watkins (some of the most influential names in contemporary British ornithology) and a whip-round of £54.

Salter instituted a reward system of payments for successful nests to induce local farmers to co-operate, a system later adopted by the RSPB in its efforts to protect other rare birds elsewhere in Britain. In 1905 E.G.B. Meade-Waldo became treasurer and visited two nests holding the first young to have been reared in ten years, and it was this gentleman and a couple of his closest friends who personally provided virtually all the cash until 1918.

In 1906 three birds were reared from a nest in the upper Towy valley, despite being photographed by Richard Kearton, and two young flew from a nest in the Usk valley. These two young southern Kites were shot in December of that year. In 1907 the Usk adults laid once more but were robbed by London collectors and never bred again. Gradually numbers built up, though those that chose to nest away from the Towy valley had little success. In 1910 five young Kites flew, but in 1911 only three. In 1912, eight years after the establishment of the Kite Committee, no less than nine pairs nested, rearing eight young between them. A youngster may also have flown from a tenth nest. So there was cause for optimism, but, as was often the case, it was short-lived.

In 1913 not a single Kite was reared and only two survived to fly in 1914. The War years brought little respite and in 1920 those involved in attempting to save this tiny remnant population must have been virtually heartbroken. The government decided to fell many woods and the lumberjacks employed for the job shot many adult Kites. Local labourers found that they could make a few pounds by taking eggs for collectors and Salter called the year a total disaster.

By 1922 the situation was as desperate as ever. The Kite Committee was back where it had started in 1904 and the Reverend D. Edmondes Owen, together with A. Gwynne-Vaughan, for seventeen years the man on the spot, could locate no more than three nests. Owen died the same year and his place was taken by another local vicar, the Reverend W.J. Constable. It was in 1922 that the RSPB Watchers' Committee first became involved and rewards due were paid on their behalf by Mrs F.E. Lemon. A local retired police inspector, A.W. Jones, was recruited and, on the basis of a £10 annual honorarium, played a considerable role in the Kite story for many years.

For several years thereafter breeding success was negligible and some of those who had worked hard and long to save the Kite as a British bird began to doubt whether the operation was worthwhile. Even trusted watchers were open to suspicion and the village policeman in Cilycwm, the Reverend Constable's own village, was caught attempting to sell a Kite's egg. One of the official watchers was actually caught trying to sell a clutch of three eggs. Finally, in 1932, a clutch of Welsh Kite's eggs was exhibited at a meeting of the august British Oologists' Association, leading to mass resignations from the Society and uproar among ornithologists.

Between 1900 and 1947 some eighty-nine Kite nests were discovered and documented. No less than twenty-one nests had been robbed, or the birds had failed to breed in suspicious circumstances. In two cases the adults had been shot, and in a further four cases disturbance by bird photographers or other visitors had caused desertion. Collectors, then, accounted for half the known failures.

About this time C.H. Gowland attempted the experiment of importing Kites' eggs from Spain to place in Buzzards' nests in an attempt to build up the population. In 1927 twenty-one eggs were distributed in Buzzards' nests in the Kite area of central Wales. Only two hatched, however, and it was a bold man who decided to persevere and import a further fifty-three eggs in 1928. This time they were dispatched by sea rather than by air and the hatching success seemed to prove the validity of the experiment. No less than thirty-one hatched and were cared for by Buzzard foster parents. However, Spanish Kites are migratory and, though young birds were seen around the area the following year, none appeared to have returned to breed.

By 1937 Constable and Mrs Lemon, both nearly eighty, had decided to retire. Constable was awarded the RSPB's Silver Medal. His place was taken by Miss Raikes of Bwlch with a budget of £100 for 1938. This extraordinary lady took things very much into her own hands. She appealed for funds and raised a further £240 for rewards in 1938. In 1939 another £310 was raised to be added to the

A Red Kite at its nest. After becoming Britain's rarest breeding bird this magnificent predator has increased and prospered in recent years, thanks to a greater public awareness of conservation.

£100 granted by the RSPB. No less than seven pairs attempted to breed, though no more than three young were reared.

The outbreak of war made travelling difficult and Miss Raikes was fortunate enough to enlist the support of Mrs I.M. Vaughan to watch over the Kites during these years. In 1945 four nests produced only four young. Two nests each produced two young. At a third nest, where eggs had been seen, there were marks of triconni nails — it had been climbed with irons and robbed. The dispossessed birds then descended the valley and interfered with a fourth nesting pair causing them to desert. So a single act had prevented the breeding of half the total British Kite population and forty years of effort had just maintained the Kite at its 1905 level. By now, Miss Raikes being incapacitated, Mrs Vaughan was carrying the whole burden of the Kite operation and her husband,

Captain H.R.H. Vaughan, proposed to the West Wales Field Society that they should take over the whole of Operation Kite.

Gradually things started to improve: in 1950 eight young Kites flew; in 1951 — eleven; in 1952 — seven; in 1953 — eleven; and in 1954 — no less than twelve. Once more there was cause for optimism, but once again disaster struck. The myxomatosis epidemic of 1954–5 that struck the rabbit population severely reduced the availability of food and in 1955 six nests produced only a single young Kite. Just as serious was the breakdown of the Kite Committee. While internal squabbles divided the members, the Vaughans carried on regardless. But it was not until 1958 that the feud was settled, largely due to the efforts of Colonel H. Morrey Salmon and Lord Hurcomb. A new Kite Committee was established under the chairmanship of Captain Vaughan, and the RSPB took over responsibility for protection and finance.

The years 1959 and 1960 showed some improvement, but then disaster struck yet again. In the two years that followed only six and eight young were reared and a large proportion of nests failed. Early in 1963 a dead Kite was found to contain large quantities of dieldrin, one of the deadly chlorinated hydrocarbons, evidently picked up from eating sheep carrion. At this time dieldrin was widely used in sheep dips. Thereafter, slowly, and with the aid of a voluntary ban, things began to improve and in 1967 no less than twenty-two pairs reared eleven young — the best figures this century. Gradually the Kite was building up its numbers under a regime of increasing protection and nest-guarding, for despite the well-known status of the species, nests were still robbed by egg collectors. No less than four nests were robbed in 1972 alone. By 1973 twenty-six pairs were present, rearing fourteen young. In 1975 a record number of twenty-four youngsters were reared, and in 1977 the number of nests passed the thirty mark for the first time, with thirty-three pairs rearing seventeen young. By now the Kite had expanded its range and could be found up to forty miles away from its main stronghold. In 1979 a record thirty-six pairs reared eighteen young, though the number of unsuccessful nests remained worryingly high. Throughout its turbulent history almost fifty percent of known nests failed to produce young. In 1969 two pairs each reared two broods of three young, the first such occurrence since 1912. Every year egg collectors account for some nests, though in 1972, for the first time, a robbed pair relaid and reared two young. There is also an increase in the number of young birds that are taken from nests, presumably to be sold to the bird collections and wildlife parks that have appeared in recent years.

This, then, is the history of a bird that came back from virtual extinction. There can be no doubt that but for the actions of a few individuals the Red Kite would have followed the White-tailed Eagle into extinction as a British breeding bird. Equally there can be little doubt that natural recolonization would have been highly unlikely. British Red Kites, unlike most of their Continental counterparts, are non-migratory and the difficulties of a reintroduction have already been noted from the attempted egg introduction of the late 1920s. However, should the present trend continue, there seems no reason why the Kite should not spread outwards from its present Welsh headquarters to reoccupy areas that were abandoned last century. Already birds have been noted in Devon and this seems by far the most likely county in England in which they will breed. Meanwhile the bird is an extremely rare wanderer to the Midlands and East Anglia.

The story of the Honey Buzzard is not really one of a bird that came back, though it was undoubtedly extinct as a breeder between 1911 and 1923. The latter date is mysterious, however, for Witherby, in *The Handbook of British Birds,* says that it was extinct until 1928, but then notes that 1923 record. Whatever the facts, there remains a period of extinction after which Honey Buzzards have returned to breed with us once more.

There can be little doubt that even in the distant past it was never a common bird. Though Britain once had more of the extensive forests favoured by the species, the summer climate is such that there is seldom the wealth of wild bees' nests necessary to support a large population. There is also little doubt that this species, too, suffered at the hands of gamekeepers and collectors, and that by 1911 it had reached a low ebb. Leslie Brown 'guesstimates' the population at never more than a score of nests and there is no evidence to contradict this opinion. Even as early as 1860 a clutch of Honey Buzzard eggs was fetching £5, while a pair with their nestlings might fetch as much as £40 — a small fortune. At this time a few pairs nested in the New Forest: not surprisingly they were extinct by 1870. Though it has bred in the past as far north as Aberdeen, it is now more or less confined to southern England. Inevitably its whereabouts have remained secret and even today it is difficult to state exactly how many pairs breed with us. Probably no one really knows. From about 1930 onwards birds returned to the New Forest and several pairs have bred annually ever since. They occasionally nest elsewhere in England and in Scotland. Probably less than a dozen pairs are involved in any one year, but this may closely match its status at any time over the past two hundred years. So the Honey Buzzard has come back from extinction, but we can hope for no more than a slow increase for what seems destined to remain a rare bird in Britain.

Apart from the White-tailed Eagle only one other species has been lost, making no permanent return during the past two hundred years. It was first described, as were so many of the world's birds, by Linnaeus in 1758, based on specimens from Egypt. Appropriately enough it was named *Charadrius alexandrinus*. In 1787 a Dr Boys collected one near Sandwich in Kent, and it was described in 1801 by Latham as *Charadrius cantianus*. However, it was later realized that the two were synonymous and the Linnaeus' name had precedence. The point of this discursion is to demonstrate just how rare the Kentish Plover has always been in Britain; as late as its discovery, less than two hundred years ago, it was confined to the area of Sandwich and nearby Pegwell Bays.

The presence of such a rare bird was too much for the early nineteenth-century collectors, who descended on the breeding grounds to collect eggs every year. In 1843 the existence of the famous Dungeness colony was disclosed by Yarrell and thereafter that area too became the happy hunting ground of the eggers. Year after year birds were shot from the nest and their eggs taken by private collectors. By 1870 no more than fifteen pairs remained and it was not until they were protected in 1905 that the situation improved, with twenty-one pairs rearing young. The following year saw forty-four pairs. Soon after, the Dungeness to Hythe miniature railway was constructed right through the middle of the main colony, and the area was invaded by Victorian bathers. Though

Named after the English county in which it most regularly bred, the Kentish Plover has managed to keep a toehold in Britain for most of this century.

Dungeness is now dominated by its nuclear power station, the visitor will also be impressed by the bungalows and chalets that have sprung up all along the coast. The disturbance to a rare breeding bird proved intolerable. Elsewhere in Kent a similar story can be told. The Kentish Plover formerly had a stronghold at Romney Hoy behind Littlestone, but here too bungalow development ruined the area and between 1904 and 1928 this colony was also exterminated. The Kentish Plovers continued breeding at Sandwich from 1932 to 1935, and at Rye Harbour from 1948 to 1955. But at Rye, coastal development in the form of caravan sites caused an increasing amount of disturbance and the last recorded breeding took place in 1956. Though politically part of Britain, the Channel Islands, where Kentish Plovers still breed, is geographically part of France.

And that would be the end of the story were it not for one of those persistent little rumours that so often pervade the bird-watching scene. Though there has been no official announcement or confirmation it seems that Kentish Plovers have been breeding in south-east England again for several years. Their location, numbers, success, etc., remain unknown — but they are there and should be left well alone. Finally, in 1979, a pair bred 'officially' on the borders of Lincolnshire and South Humberside, and a pair and two chicks were present on 10 July.

Prior to the Second World War, colonies of Bearded Tits were few and the population was far from secure. We can only guess at its numbers prior to the drainage of the Fens. Reed beds certainly existed in plenty and, being in the right geographical position in eastern England, undoubtedly held these birds. But whether they were really plentiful is open to doubt. Bearded Tits, as we have seen in recent years, are particularly prone to hard winters, and their numbers drop dramatically when the reed beds, and particularly the reed follicles, are frozen. A series of mild winters may boost their numbers dramatically, for they are prolific breeders, rearing three or even four broods each of five to seven young in a season. By the autumn even a small population of adults can multiply several times over. In the early 1960s, for example, my friend David Pearson estimated the autumn population of the Westwood Marshes at Walberswick at over a thousand birds. Nevertheless the bitter winters of 1962 and 1963 reduced them to a handful of pairs in that locality.
    Drainage reduced the available habitat throughout the nineteenth century and collectors of skins and eggs put further pressure on an already scarce bird. The going rate for a skin was four shillings during the latter part of the last century; a similar amount was paid for a dozen eggs, or for a live pair imported from Holland. They were, at that time, an exotic addition to the cage bird trade, though, being difficult to feed, most perished. They disappeared from county after county in southern England, until by 1930 they were found only in Norfolk and, in smaller numbers, in Suffolk. At that time they had a stronghold among the Broads in the Hickling and Horsey area, where that famed ornithologist Jim Vincent estimated there were thirty pairs. Adding a similar number in the neighbour-

A male Bearded Tit at an East Anglian nest hidden deep at the foot of a reed bed. Despite fluctuating numbers this frost-prone bird has survived to flourish in recent years.

ing Broads, a total of well under a hundred pairs existed — and that was in a good year. In Suffolk even fewer nested, and the bird was extinct at Slapton Ley in Devon, previously noted as a regular haunt.

Then came the war and the creation of new habitats along the Suffolk coast and the virtually total cessation of collecting. Soon there were more Bearded Tits than ever before. By the time that bird-watchers were allowed access to the coastal marshes of Suffolk after 1945, the Bearded Tit population was at an all-time high. The subsequent bitter winter of early 1947 caused their numbers to plummet. During the next breeding season only three pairs could be found in the whole of the country — all at Minsmere. The entire population of Bearded Tits in Europe had been estimated at no more than a hundred pairs. Yet recovery was rapid and overall numbers continued to grow. In 1959 the build-up in population and a splendid breeding season caused a massive eruption of birds from their Norfolk and Suffolk strongholds, aided by a huge immigration from the vast reed beds of Holland, where 20,000 birds were estimated in late summer. Early in the mornings small flocks of 'Beardies' could be seen gathered among the reed tops before flying high into the air uttering their distinctive 'pting' notes in a state of high excitement. Soon they were being recorded from all parts of the country, in areas as diverse as large reed beds and narrow reed-fringed dykes. Some birds may have returned whence they came, but many stayed on to form new colonies in Humberside, the Norfolk coast, Essex, Kent, Hampshire and Dorset. By 1972 the total population was put at four hundred pairs — the largest total ever recorded for the species.

Though there can be no doubt that the incidental provision of marshes as a result of wartime defensive flooding offered the Bearded Tit a home where none had been before, equally there were other factors at work. Chief of these was the climatic amelioration which has affected many other species. During the warmer winters that followed 1963 the population of Bearded Tits built up, extended and consolidated its colonization. The Dutch birds that invaded Britain in 1959 also moved eastwards to Denmark, where the population had built up to over a hundred pairs by 1968. Sweden was first colonized in 1966 and within ten years the birds had moved northwards to the huge reed beds at Lake Tåkern in central Sweden and as far as Lake Roxen.

Even today in England, however, egg collectors still take their toll of this species, undaunted by the law and by the location of nests inside the apparently protective boundaries of nature reserves. The cutting of reeds for thatch continues, and may even be increasing as short-stemmed cereal production makes less straw available. Severe winters still decimate the population, but the species' power of recovery is staggering and their now known migratory behaviour will doubtless prevent their extinction in the foreseeable future.

The Red Kite, Honey Buzzard, Kentish Plover and Bearded Tit have all come back from the brink of extinction. Without exception it was a brink created by man, and in most cases the result of direct persecution. The respite of two world wars may have been a significant factor, but in reading their stories one cannot help but be impressed by the role played by a few individuals in guarding and protecting these birds. To them all we owe a great debt — they were truly the founders of the modern British conservation movement.

Chapter Six

Symbol of Success

It is not difficult to imagine the thrill experienced by two Suffolk bird-watchers who discovered that the Avocet had returned to their county to breed in 1947 on the marshy floods of the recently inundated coast. From 1813, when it was drained, until the outbreak of war in 1939, the area, intersected by drainage ditches with levels controlled by sluices to the sea, was used as summer grazing for sheep and cattle. Reeds fringed the ditches and Yellow Wagtails and Sedge Warblers bred in abundance. In winter splashy patches developed and a few duck joined the throngs of Lapwings and Golden Plovers. Then, fearing an invasion, the War Office requisitioned the fields and in June 1940 the freshwater outlet sluice was closed and the sea water inlet opened. When the whole area had been flooded both sluices were closed and the Minsmere levels remained flooded until 1945 and the end of hostilities. Meanwhile the floods had been colonized by reeds, and a total of four hundred acres of marshland developed at one of the most strategic sites in Britain. Strategic, that is, not only in dissuading the enemy from invading this particular stretch of coastline but in creating a wetland where none had existed for over half a century and within a hundred miles of the bird-rich marshes just across the North Sea in Holland. Reed beds inland and salty marshy splashes near the sea wall offered a wealth of habitats that had virtually disappeared from southern and eastern England.

During the war Minsmere remained in military hands and was used as a training ground. To bird-watchers it was strictly out of bounds, but to birds the newly-created marshes must have been a paradise. We can only imagine the colonization by marsh-loving warblers, by Bearded Tits and by Bitterns, all of which were established by the time that bird-watchers were once again allowed access. Then on 8 April 1947 Brigadier H.M. Stanford and his brother, Lieutenant-Colonel J.K. Stanford, waded out across one of the pools to see whether the Avocets had indeed laid eggs.

It was Brigadier Stanford who first suspected that Avocets might be breeding at Minsmere and announced with an air of casual *sang-froid* to his brother 'I think we ought to find an Avocet's nest tomorrow.' J.K. Stanford takes up the story:

> As we came down the slope of the hill above the marshes, I heard a shrill cry which was new to me from a mere beyond the fringe of the reed-beds, and saw four or five Avocets flying. We picked our way round the mere and sat down on a bank in a quiet spot to watch them. A few minutes later one bird was sitting on a little mud island near the western edge of the mere.
>
> We watched her for twenty minutes and then my brother said, 'I'm going to wade out and have a look.' It seemed hours while he did so but the birds were unmistakably anxious. At last he came wading back to me, slowly and with an expressionless face.
>
> 'Is there a nest there?' I asked.
>
> 'Three!' was the reply. 'You'd better go and look.'
>
> I could not believe my ears and could, indeed, hardly believe my eyes, when I had waded out myself knee-deep through that shallow water which was still pocked with the mortar-bomb craters of a wartime battle school. But here on the islet of mud were the three nests with eggs, each within a few yards of the other.

Immediately a dawn to dusk watch was instituted by the land-owner Captain Stuart Ogilvie, the Stanford brothers and Major E. Lynn-Allen — an array of military brass that boasted two MCs and which must be unique in ornithological annals. Four pairs of Avocets bred that season, watched over by this small band of dedicated volunteers. Unbeknown to them, however, a further four or five pairs had been discovered at Havergate Island, a dozen or so miles south along the Suffolk coast, on 6 July, by Mr F.M. Hollis.

A similar round-the-clock-watching operation was instituted by Philip Brown of the RSPB, together with the discoverer and the guardian T.D. Harvey. It is astonishing just how well the secrets were kept, for rumour has it that each group was unaware of the other's existence.

The history of the Avocet in Britain is a tale of persecution and destruction. In the seventeenth century the great field naturalist

The Avocet, or awl-bird as it was once known, was too obvious to survive the collectors of the last century. Its return in the 1940s is a classic conservation story.

John Ray described it as not uncommon along the east coast, while in the eighteenth century Thomas Pennant wrote 'We have seen them in considerable numbers in the breeding season near Rossdike Wash, in Lincolnshire.' By 1837 William Yarrell was able to write that it had been some years since more than twenty Avocets a month had been offered for sale in Leadenhall Market, though he himself had recently found them nesting in marshes near Rye.

Undoubtedly Norfolk had been the species' major stronghold, with well-established colonies at Salthouse, Winterton, Horsey and on the Bure near Seven Mile House. All had been ruthlessly exterminated either directly by collectors, or by local fensmen with an eye to the 'collector market', by 1824. In Lincolnshire, near the Humber, it lingered until 1836, and Yarrell's colony on the Romney Marshes near Rye was gone by 1842 or 1843. This was, with one exception, the last recorded nesting in Britain for nearly a hundred years. In Suffolk itself the Avocet bred until 1818 at Orford, but was thereafter only an irregular visitor until a pair laid eggs at Thorpe Mere in 1882. They were 'collected'.

The Avocet was never a common or widespread breeding bird in Britain. Its particular habitat requirements of shallow muddy water with a high degree of salinity, close to bare, low-lying marshy islands, could never have been common. Drainage of suitable coastal marshes, the straightening of rivers and the reclamation of estuaries must have reduced its numbers well before the collectors got to work. Nevertheless, it is not unreasonable to presume that towards the end of the eighteenth century its several colonies were still strong and healthy. It did not take long for the collectors of eggs and skins to polish off such a highly-localized and colonial bird. The Reverend C.A. Johns wrote

'This bird has become so rare, that having recently applied to several collectors in Norfolk . . . to know if they could procure me a specimen, I was told by one that they were not seen oftener than once in seven years — by the other . . . that if attainable at all [it] could not be purchased for less than five pounds.

At the time he was writing, in 1909, five pounds was a hefty sum indeed.

Then in 1938 two pairs bred, almost certainly successfully, at the then intertidal Tacumshin Lake in south-eastern Ireland, a country where it had occurred less than a score of times as a vagrant. It seemed, at the time, to be no more than a freak occurrence. In 1941 a pair laid three eggs at Salthouse in Norfolk which were 'collected', but in 1944 chicks were noted in Essex. In 1946 a clutch of eggs was once again collected from a Norfolk site. On the evidence of breeding by at least eight pairs rearing nine young at Minsmere and Havergate in 1947, it may be assumed that these birds, despite their large size and bold black and white plumage, had probably nested unnoticed along the Suffolk coast, protected by an disinterested military occupation. Perhaps the wartime breeding in Norfolk and Essex was simply a spin-off of an earlier Suffolk colonization, of a similar type to the sporadic breedings from Lincolnshire to Kent, reports of which have peppered the post-war years.

At present only three major colonies exist in Britain: at Minsmere, Havergate and at the more recently established Cley Marshes
in Norfolk. Over the past thirty years the Avocet population has
increased from seven to only a hundred and fifty pairs, indicating
both the lack of suitable breeding sites and the ceaseless persecution
by egg collectors of all rare birds that are foolish enough to attempt
breeding outside the confines of a strictly protected nature reserve.

At Minsmere, site of the first discovered 1947 breeding colony,
1948 was a disappointment. Eight birds returned in April, but their
breeding pools had shrunk, plants had colonized larger areas and
there may also have been a diminishing supply of food in a less
saline environment. The birds displayed in a half-hearted way,
never settled and were gone before the end of the month. The hopes
of the anxious watchers were crushed. No Avocets were to breed
again at Minsmere until 1963, by which time active management of
the area had created the now famous 'Scrape'.

Meanwhile the then tiny RSPB had negotiated the lease of Minsmere, and set out to make an outright purchase of Havergate Island.
The watchers who had set themselves up at Minsmere and had
suffered such disappointment immediately transferred to Havergate and set up camp on 1 May. Colonel J.K. Stanford, Philip
Brown of the RSPB and Dick Wolfendale, the Society's watcher,
settled in for the duration of the Avocets' nesting. Five pairs were
soon incubating, but after ten days one clutch disappeared overnight. Then, within a few days of hatching, on 18 May, a clutch was
taken by rats. On 21 May a further clutch disappeared. One clutch
hatched but the four chicks died of exposure when rain and hail-
storms struck the coast. Two pairs relaid, but one of these clutches
was taken by rats and, at the end of the season, only three young
Avocets flew. Fortunately four more pairs bred on the nearby Lantern Marshes, in company with a colony of Black-headed Gulls.
Rats were present here too, but the aggressiveness of the Black-
headed Gulls kept predation down and ten Avocet chicks flew.

Having acquired Havergate and, with the co-operation of the
Infestation Control Division of the Ministry of Agriculture, taken
steps to eradicate the rat menace, the RSPB looked forward to the
1949 breeding season with cautious optimism. Early April was the
time scheduled for Avocet arrival, but on 1 March an exceptionally

high spring tide breached the island's walls in a dozen places and washed away the sluice that controlled the water level. Minsmere had proved unsuitable and the Lantern Marshes had been partially drained during the winter. Havergate offered the only hope for the Avocets, due to return within five weeks, and that was under four feet of water.

In a mad race against time the walls were temporarily rebuilt with pick and shovel. The sluice was repaired, but even at the end of the month there was still a foot of water covering the breeding islets. Fortunately the Avocets returned a little late and on 4 April Philip Brown and my old friend G.B.G. Benson saw the first birds at the mouth of Butley Creek. As if to celebrate RSPB ownership all the Avocets returned to Havergate, along with five hundred pairs of Black-headed Gulls.

No less than seventeen pairs of Avocets bred and, under the watchful eyes of the voluntary wardens, reared over thirty chicks. Slowly but surely, and despite numerous disasters and problems including massive flooding in 1953, the number of pairs and total of chicks successfully reared grew year by year. The summer of 1951 saw twenty-four pairs of Avocets. By 1955 no less than sixty-six pairs reared a hundred young, and in 1957 some ninety-seven pairs bred — a peak that was not to be approached again for several years to come.

In 1958 numbers actually declined, followed by further decreases in 1959 and 1960, when under seventy pairs bred. For several seasons prior to 1958 the number of chicks reared had declined, largely due to predation by the fast-growing colony of Black-headed Gulls that had multiplied four times during the previous ten years. While the presence of the gulls had undoubtedly provided a protective umbrella during the early years, now their predation of young Avocets and competition for restricted nest sites was proving harmful. There was evidence that the continual evaporation of salt water on Havergate had increased salinity to a particularly high level and eliminated much Avocet food. For preference these birds choose brackish, rather than pure salt, water in which to feed and,

Opposite. *The Honey Buzzard has never had more than a toehold in southern England, but it has been a toehold to which it has clung tenaciously throughout the last hundred years.*

like a salt pan in the warmer climes of the Mediterranean, Havergate had become too salty. Wells were drilled and fresh water pumped into the lagoons to attempt to produce the correct brackish mix. The nests of gulls were destroyed by a variety of methods and eventually the Black-headeds moved away completely. There were, perhaps, sufficient Avocets to protect themselves against predators without the aid of the gulls.

Breeding Avocets in Suffolk

Number of Pairs (Number of Young Reared)

Year	Havergate		Minsmere	Elsewhere
1947	4	(8)	4 (1)	-
1948	5	(13)	1 (0)	-
1949	17	(31)	-	-
1950	21	(40)	-	-
1951	24	(40)	-	-
1952	40	(120)	-	-
1953	45	(67)	-	-
1954	52	(c.70)	-	-
1955	66	(c.100)	-	-
1956	79	(c.50)	-	-
1957	97	(c.50)	-	-
1958	90	(31)	-	-
1959	65	(44)	-	-
1960	67	(35)	-	-
1961	62	(60)	-	-
1962	77	(20)	-	1
1963	55	(29)	1 (1)	-

1	2
3	

1 Photograhed in camouflaged display, in which it attempts to merge with its reedy background, the Bittern has returned to breed in Britain, though its status remains at risk.
2 A Black-tailed Godwit turns its eggs prior to settling down to incubation. Once served at feasts by the hundred, it was forced into extinction by simple human greed, but has now returned.
3 Ruff at their communal lek offered an opportunity to the bird trappers of the last century that was too good to miss. Left in peace they have now re-established themselves in several areas.

Year	Havergate		Minsmere		Elsewhere	
1964	48	(52)	1	(3)	-	
1965	52	(78)	3	(10)	-	
1966	65	(124)	4	(8)	-	
1967	73	(139)	6	(16)	-	
1968	108	(162)	7	(7)	1	(1)
1969	118	(178)	11	(21)	3	(1)
1970	102	(175)	15	(34)	4	(2)
1971	93	(103)	25	(55)	7	(3)
1972	110	(25)	38	(66)	4	(1)
1973	112	(50)	38	(66)	4	(1)
1974	86	(6)	40	(57)	7	(2)
1975	107	(80)	41	(62)	9	(4)
1976	95	(12)	51	(46)	3	(0)
1977	84	(1)	53	(3)	4	(6)
1978	93	(56)	47	(19)	5	(?)
1979	95	(6)	44	(63)	8	(30)

By 1963 the colony was on the mend once more and a single pair arrived late and bred at Minsmere. During the previous winter the RSPB and its warden, Bert Axell, had set to work with bulldozers to recreate the shoreline pools that had been a feature of the area in its earliest post-war years, but which had been largely overgrown by vegetation. An acre and a half of useless coarse grass had been 'scraped' bare to form a lagoon, with three hurriedly constructed islands. On one of these a pair of Avocets settled on 22 May 1963 and hatched four young. Three chicks were taken by a Heron and one survived. The following year, 1964, Avocets once again returned to Minsmere, this time to a fourteen-acre 'Scrape' with fourteen islands from which to choose. But only one pair remained to breed. In 1965 again only a single pair returned to an even larger 'Scrape' (by then the working name had stuck for good) with even more islands for nesting birds.

That Bert Axell and his workers had been successful was never doubted. From the first year birds had started to colonize the artificial islands and now, three seasons on, there were established colonies of Black-headed Gulls, Common Terns, and even Little Terns, finally dissuaded from nesting on the open beach where season after season their eggs were destroyed by an ever-increasing public. Success, then, was never doubted, but the thrill engendered by the successful nesting of a pair of Avocets in the first season was tempered by two years of disappointment that no regular colony had become established. Then on May Day 1965 a second pair arrived, to be followed by a third a week or so later. Now there were three pairs. Slowly, year by year, the Avocet colony increased, reaching forty-seven pairs in 1978, though in that year only nineteen young were reared.

Along the way all manner of problems had to be dealt with, including a fox that evidently found Avocet eggs an irresistible delicacy and began systematically raiding the Scrape every night. To deal with the menace Bert Axell waded in total darkness among the islands he had constructed and shot the raider with a shotgun to which he had lashed a flashlight. Every bird on the Scrape took to the air in a mad and noisy panic, but all were back in their places at first light as if nothing had happened.

Even Minsmere, perhaps the best-known bird reserve in the country, is not immune from the ultimate human predator — the egg collector. One year Axell found human footprints in the mud leading directly to an Avocet nesting island. Two clutches were missing. Thereafter an all-night vigil was instituted during the critical incubation period, a procedure that has remained standard to the present time. Armed with a spotlight, watchers remain alert all through the night from vantage points that are changed on a random basis. Today it is as difficult to break into Minsmere during the egg period as it was to break out of Colditz Castle. The penalties for being caught may not be as severe, but I would not like to be an egger caught by a team of wardens passionate enough about their birds to give up their nights to guard nests. A prolonged ducking would seem likely to be the least of the thief's problems.

Havergate, meanwhile, began a steady recovery back to its old self. Freshwater pumping, the creating of a further lagoon, together with the elimination of the gull menace, enabled the colony to grow once more. As at Minsmere, however, the growth was slow, indicating perhaps that each was dependent on its success in rearing young, rather than on immigration, for its growth. There is little doubt that the initial colonization of Suffolk stemmed from Dutch colonies that had been displaced by flooding during the war. What is also clear is that the chances of birds surviving their first winter are remarkably slim. Of thirty-four chicks ringed at Minsmere in 1970, two were shot in Spain. Many more Dutch ringed birds have been recovered by similar means in France, Spain and Portugal, indicating, as clearly as could be, that simply to protect a bird in its breeding quarters is inadequate unless it can also be protected at migration stop-over points, and in its winter quarters. In view of the enormous toll that is still taken along the western seaboard of Europe, it is surprising that the Avocet population of Britain is in as healthy a state as it is.

From 1947 to the time of writing, Avocets have nested at a variety of other sites in eastern England between Lincolnshire and Kent. With a single exception only one or two pairs have been involved and no colony has lasted more than a year or two. Unfortunately, most of these sites must remain secret, for there is always a chance that the birds may return, and that egg collectors may even purchase this book. It is, however, highly unlikely that a colony of Avocets will ever establish itself outside the boundaries of a nature reserve, or that, as the case of Minsmere illustrates, they will be left in peace by collectors unless guarded day and night. In 1954 two pairs laid eggs at Buss Creek, behind Southwold, to the north of Minsmere. Both were taken, and soon after the area, which was a splendid if tiny wetland, was drained for agriculture. It is now just a rough damp mess.

In the 1970s Avocets at last became more than irregular visitors to the marshes of north Norfolk, breeding at a couple of sites. At one of these, the old-established Norfolk Naturalists' Trust Reserve at Cley, four pairs nested in 1977 and reared six young. In 1978 there were five pairs, and in 1979 eight pairs reared a total of thirty young — an exceptionally high success rate. Thus it seems that we finally have three viable colonies of Avocets in Britain, after thirty years of battling with the elements and a great deal of hard work and dedication by members and staff of the RSPB and others, who have watched over and guarded the birds day and night in their fight to maintain a toehold in this country. Not surprisingly the RSPB adopted the Avocet as its emblem — it is a pity that there are not as many wild birds to be seen as there are blue-backed plastic ones stuck to the back windows of cars.

Chapter Seven

Back to the Reeds

If the success story of the return of the Avocet is the most dramatic of the events that took place along the war-created marshes of the Suffolk coast, it must not be thought that it is the only one. Several other species, once common enough among the marshes of England, followed a similar road to local extinction during the nineteenth century. Others had been reduced to the point where they hovered on the verge of such extinction. The Ruff, Black-tailed Godwit, Black Tern and Bittern were locally extinct, while the Marsh Harrier clung precariously to a toehold in Norfolk. The creation of coastal marshes at Minsmere and nearby Walberswick offered new opportunities to all of these birds, but to none more than the Bittern and Marsh Harrier. The prerequisite of each is a large undisturbed reed bed. While Avocets may well have been tolerant of the military presence during the wartime occupation of the Suffolk coast, it seems unlikely that the Harrier would have put up with the bombs and bullets that such presence involved.

The association between Bitterns and reed beds is complete — the birds simply cannot exist without them. Cryptically coloured in browns and creams, they merge with the dead reeds of the previous season and even have a sky-pointing posture when alarmed, that effectively shows the striped chest and neck as reeds. As the reeds swing this way and that with the wind so the Bittern moves from side to side in this sky-pointing posture. If, as in a hard winter, a Bittern is disturbed in the open it will adopt this disguise instantly, whether its background is camouflaging reeds or a green lawn against which it stands out like a sore thumb and simply looks silly. In its element it is a secretive bird that would be easily overlooked were it not for its curious 'song', which consists of a repeated booming note similar to the distant foghorn of a ship at sea. It flies but seldom, and then not very far. For the Bittern a large sheltering reed bed is the complete home.

From the late eighteenth century onwards the Bittern had been in decline. The passion for draining marshes destroyed thousands of acres of prime reed beds, particularly in East Anglia where the Bittern had always had its headquarters. It was once quite widespread, however, with good numbers also in Yorkshire, Lancashire, Wales and in parts of Scotland. Even as far west as Ireland it was breeding in Ulster, Connaught and Munster, though it ceased doing so by 1840.

Drainage was undoubtedly the main cause of decline, but roast Bittern had always been a favourite fenland dish and large numbers were regularly shot for the pot. In his *Breviary of Suffolk*, published in 1618, Robert Royce was able to say:

> of our wilde fowles the partridge, pheasant, woodcock, ring dove, turtle dove, quails, larks, lapwings, plover, bitterns, bustard . . . and such like . . . afford the good housewife a dainty supply.

By 1820 the Bittern was scarce in Suffolk and by 1836 it was extinct. A small population lingered on in Norfolk until 1850, but then it succumbed there too. The collector had taken over where the fensman and drainage engineer had left off. Thereafter the bird remained no more than a winter visitor in irregular numbers, but the welcome was always the same. In the winter of 1830–1, for example, Yarrell notes that exceptional numbers of specimens were obtained, an influx the effects of which were evident as far north as Scotland, where the bird preservers of Edinburgh had obtained many more than usual. Seago in his *Birds of Norfolk* says that between 1850 and 1866 no less than a hundred Bitterns were shot in the winter months: while at Orford in Suffolk thirteen were shot and one caught by a dog in January 1848. Even so it managed to breed on two occasions, the last in 1886.

For the next twenty-five years there is no proof of Bitterns breeding in Britain, though booming was heard among the Norfolk Broads in 1900 and in Suffolk in 1901. Then in 1911 it bred near Sutton Broad; in Suffolk in 1916; and at Hickling in 1917. By 1918 there were about nine pairs in the Broads, mostly in the Hickling — Horsey area. Perhaps once again we can thank the peace that came to the marshes as a result of the fensmen going to war, for the safe return of another of our lost birds. Certainly by 1928 about twenty-five pairs were once again breeding among the Norfolk

Broads and in the following year the Bittern colonized Thorpe Fen in Suffolk despite severe spring frosts. That same season also produced a bird booming in Hampshire. By the mid-1930s it was breeding at several coastal sites, including one just outside Lowestoft and another among the Dunwich Marshes. Meanwhile in Norfolk it had spread outwards from Broadland and reached the north coast at Cley in 1937. The same year produced the only Scottish boomer of the century and the first at Leighton Moss in Lancashire. Then, just as all seemed to be going so well, the severe winters of 1938–40 struck and the population was decimated. Bitterns are dependent on eels and amphibians for food and when the marshes freeze up solid they are unable to feed. All was not lost, however, for the wartime peace of the deserted marshes enabled the Bittern to boom once again. It was at this time that it colonized the newly-created marshes of the Suffolk coast.

Despite a further setback during the winter of 1947, a survey of Bitterns in Norfolk in 1954 revealed sixty booming males, while in Suffolk there were eleven at Minsmere with others present at six different sites. Add some fifteen or so pairs outside East Anglia and a British total of just over eighty pairs was established in 1954.

So, due to a wartime respite in hunting, the growing prevalence of a new conservation-minded attitude during the present century and the creation of new habitat, the Bittern returned from extinction to reach a peak in the 1950s. At this time there were instances in Lincolnshire, where breeding was first proved in 1949, in Hampshire, and at Leighton Moss as far away as Lancashire. After years of booming, breeding was finally proved at this site in 1958. Thereafter the population increased steadily, reaching a peak of ten boomers in 1970. Almost as far away from the East Anglian stronghold is North Wales, where booming was heard in 1955 and breeding proved in 1968. Bitterns were heard in Somerset in the late 1950s and became regular breeders soon after, though the total of two pairs in 1970 was probably seldom exceeded. Nearer at hand, Kent was colonized during the war, though breeding was not proved (in the Stour Valley) until 1948. By the early 1960s there were nine booming males present in the county. Breeding or booming confirmed the presence of birds as far away as Northumberland from 1956 to 1960 and in 1962 in Ireland and Yorkshire, but these were to prove isolated occurrences.

Persecuted by collectors and sought for the cooking pot, the Bittern was destroyed mainly by the drainage of its reed marsh habitat. Now it has returned, though its future is far from secure.

Following the abandonment of Cley Marshes on the North Nor-folk coast in 1963, where there had been four pairs in the 1950s, Michael Seago organized a repeat Bittern census in 1970. The results were startling: numbers in the Broads had crashed from sixty boomers in 1954 to twenty-seven in 1970. At Minsmere numbers remained steady, for the coypu was already recognized as a menace and its numbers controlled.

Minsmere, however, was also home to the RSPB's 'Operation Bittern' in 1963, when Britain was held in the grip of ice and snow for weeks on end. Half-starved Bitterns from all over the country were sent to the reserve to be fed and cared for by Bert Axell and his staff before being released on the marshes. At this time one was even caught queuing at a London bus stop.

Elsewhere in the country the census actually showed some increase, and the total for Britain as a whole showed a decline of only just over ten percent, all accounted for by the serious decline in Norfolk.

Only six years later the picture had changed radically — and for the worse. Kent and South Wales had been abandoned. Lincolnshire and North Wales were down to only a pair or two each and the total in the Broads had slumped to only ten boomers with not a singleton at Hickling — the first year of total absence since 1917. Lancashire, meanwhile, had maintained its population at ten (including nine at Leighton Moss), while in Suffolk Bitterns had actually increased from sixteen or seventeen in 1970 to twenty-one or twenty-two booming males. The grand total for the whole country amounted to only forty-five to forty-seven males.

From a peak of seventy-nine to eighty-three pairs in 1954 the Bittern population had declined to sixty-eight to seventy-two pairs in 1970 and forty-five to forty-seven pairs in 1976. In 1977 it was considered rare enough to merit the attention of the *British Birds'* Rare Breeding Birds Panel, which noted a total of forty booming males. The decline was most obvious in Norfolk, where no more than eight could be found. Elsewhere it was present at one site in Kent; at Leighton Moss in Lancashire, where eleven were booming; in Lincolnshire and Humberside; at Minsmere, where seven compared with thirteen in 1976; at another Suffolk site where eight boomers were present; and in two other counties which have perforce to remain nameless on security grounds.

Thus the Bittern, having returned from extinction, is once more in decline, even, it seems, in the strictly preserved nature reserves operated by the RSPB. Hard weather certainly has reduced the numbers of this species and the bitter winters of 1947 and of 1962 and 1963 took a heavy toll. Estimates in Holland put the kill as high as twenty-three percent in 1955–6, but the Bittern does seem to be able to make a comparatively quick recovery from such setbacks and it is generally felt that such mortalities are not the cause of the recent decline. Indeed the mild winters of the 1970s would seem to have offered a major opportunity to the Bittern to increase its numbers quite considerably.

The decline has also been linked to the increasing number of coypus to be found in East Anglia. First released during the last war when their value, as producers of the fur nutria, was slashed, these large South American rodents increased and prospered in Broadland, reaching a peak of 200,000 in 1963. Severe winters then reduced their numbers dramatically, but they have staged a remarkable recovery and are once again a considerable (and expensive) pest. Their link with the decline of certain Broadland birds, including Great Crested Grebes and Marsh Harriers, as well as Bitterns, is circumstantial. They may trample over nests, they certainly keep waterways open and may even graze reed beds to produce new areas of open water, but there is no direct evidence linking their activities with the decline of the Bittern. Reed-cutting for thatch has also been suggested as a possible cause of the decline. But, once again, there is no direct evidence. Most of the marshes where Bitterns breed have been cut over for many years and the area of open water thus created may actually benefit the species. If, however, the cutting, and especially subsequent burning, continues late into the spring, then the disturbance alone may prevent Bitterns, as well as other marshland birds, from breeding.

The evidence points to one significant factor — the increasing pollution and disturbance of the Broads. Eutrophication, combined with increasing turbidity as a result of more and more pleasure boats, may have seriously affected the fauna and flora of the Broads with a consequent effect on the population of fish. The implications of such a decline for the Bittern, as well as other fish-eaters such as the Grey Heron, are obvious. The loss of reed edge, an area favoured by feeding Bitterns, together with a growth of sedge and other scrub as a result of wave action, may also be involved.

Strange as it may seem, the species is still persecuted by egg collectors who, to my knowledge, still raid the second Suffolk site almost every year. However, there is nothing new in this: these marshes have proved a happy hunting ground for such vandals for years; years during which the Bittern increased and prospered. Here, then, is a bird that came back, but which may well be lost again.

A similar swing of fortune has affected the Marsh Harrier, a bird

A male Marsh Harrier approaches its nest with a bream in one foot and a ring on the other. Undisturbed reed beds are essential if this delightful predator is to survive.

that was widespread in Britain and Ireland in the 1800s, but which suffered on a number of different fronts. Indeed, so formidable were the forces lined up against this species that the wonder is that it survived for so long and that it was so quick and tenacious in its comeback. Not only did the Harrier face the same threats to its breeding habitat presented by the nineteenth-century desire to drain every marsh in sight, but it also had to contend with the newly-established sport of shooting game and the gamekeepers who saw their job as the elimination of all 'vermin' with hooked bills. That Marsh Harriers do take young Partridges and Pheasants cannot be doubted. Today, however, we are able to put their depredations into perspective, for they have little significant effect on game populations when compared with other factors such as the weather. Nevertheless, they were ruthlessly shot by gamekeepers during the early part of last century and by 1837 Yarrell was only able to cite Devon and Norfolk as regular breeding areas. By then, of course, the now rare Marsh Harrier was much sought after by the collectors and by 1870 it was restricted to a single area of Broadland. In 1878 it was extinct. In Ireland, a country much more suited to its needs, it was 'the most abundant of our larger birds of prey and widely distributed' according to Watters, writing in 1853. By 1900 it was decidedly rare and the last pair bred in 1917.

After 1878 the Marsh Harrier was proved to breed on only six occasions in England prior to 1926 — a period of fifty years of virtual extinction. It was, however, at Hickling in Norfolk that most of these sporadic attempts at nesting were made and it was to Hickling that the birds eventually returned. From 1927 onwards four pairs attempted to breed each year, protected by the land-owner Lord Desborough and later by the embryonic Norfolk Naturalists' Trust. Hickling remained the stronghold, though Major Anthony Buxton also protected those that chose to nest at nearby Horsey during the same period.

Once again it was the wartime flooding of the coastal marshes that created habitat enabling the Marsh Harrier to return to breed in Suffolk for the first time in a hundred years. F.C. Cook saw birds carrying nesting materials in 1942, but was unable to prove breeding until he discovered a nest near Lowestoft in 1945. In 1946 three pairs were present along the coast and by 1958 they reached a peak of eight nests, rearing a total of twelve young in four separate marshes. In 1960 the number declined to five nests in Suffolk, while in Norfolk none bred at all. Thereafter the Suffolk coast remained the species' stronghold, if that is an appropriate term for a bird that had reached such a low ebb.

For several seasons in the 1960s Minsmere was the Marsh Harrier's only breeding site in Britain and there it was reduced to a single young male supporting two nesting females. A variety of causes have been offered in explanation of the decline, including the presence of coypus, attacks on eggs and young by Bitterns, the heavy slaughter of migrants along the coasts of France and Spain, and simply the contraction in numbers that any species will experience at the very edge of its range. There can be no doubt that the fortunes of our East Anglian Marsh Harriers are closely tied up with the fortunes of Harriers in nearby Holland, where hundreds, if not thousands, of pairs can be found on the reclaimed polders of the former Zuider Zee.

Whatever the causes, the Marsh Harrier has made another gradual comeback and occupied more of its former haunts during the 1970s. In 1977 no less than sixteen to seventeen pairs were reported, rearing a total of forty-four young, the best season during the present century. By this time birds had returned to Norfolk and had spread outwards to Humberside, Kent and Lancashire. Nevertheless Suffolk remained the headquarters with eight nests, including four at Minsmere.

The number of pairs that can exist in these islands is strictly limited by the number of available reed beds. A marsh of even three or four hundred acres is unlikely to support more than three or four pairs of Harriers and there are few unoccupied marshes of that size in south-east England. Elsewhere the Harrier has bred in Wales on occasion and in north-west England, but here, too, undisturbed reed beds are decidedly scarce. Given a succession of good breeding seasons and, perhaps, a continued abundance in Holland creating a surplus of young birds, the Marsh Harrier could no doubt spread to several other parts of the country. What is certain is that it could never regain its former abundance and is destined unfortunately to remain a rare bird.

Though the establishment of these coastal marshes suited the Avocet, Bittern and Marsh Harrier in their recolonization, they were not the only species to benefit. The reed beds were soon alive with Reed, Sedge and Grasshopper Warblers, and with Coots, Moorhens and the elusive Water Rail. Soon they were to be home to another bird that came back.

When Savi's Warbler was first discovered breeding at Stodmarsh in Kent in 1960, it was the first record of its doing so in Britain for over a hundred years. During that time it had remained a scarce vagrant, often perhaps overlooked, but nevertheless decidedly rare. In view of its Reed Warbler-like appearance and Grasshopper Warbler-like song, this is not perhaps so surprising and certainly its early history in this country is clouded by the difficulty with which it was to be identified.

The first record was of one shot in mid-May, probably in 1819,

A distinctive, low-pitched reeling distinguishes Savi's from the more common Grasshopper Warbler. Never widespread, it is a recolonist that seems well established in southern and eastern England.

in Norfolk. The specimen was sent to the famous ornithologist Temminck, who untypically failed to identify it as a new species and thus missed the chance of having his name added to that of a warbler. He had already got Temminck's Stint, Temminck's Horned Lark, Temminck's Courser and others to his credit. In 1824 Savi recognized it as an undescribed species identical to specimens obtained in his native Italy, and so added his name to ornithological history and nomenclature.

Having been recognized, Savi's Warbler was to enjoy but a short history as a British breeding bird. Its Fenland haunts in Cambridgeshire and Huntingdonshire were centred on Baitsbight, Milton, Burwell, Wicken and Woodwalton, according to Alfred Newton. Within a few years most were drained and Savi's Warbler, or the Red Night-reeler as it was locally known, was confined to a few areas of Norfolk where the last British bird was shot at Surlingham Broad in June 1856. Collectors may have made the final *coup de grace* but drainage was a more important factor, and there is some contemporary evidence of decline and contraction of range throughout Europe.

This contraction of range, a phenomenon that affects many, if not most birds at some time or another, was followed by an expansion during the middle of the twentieth century that brought fresh areas within the species' range. It was noted in Sweden in 1944, as increasing in Germany and France by 1950, and a male summered at Wicken Fen in 1954. During the late 1950s birds were noted at an area of mining subsidence along the Kentish River Stour east of Canterbury, near the village of Stodmarsh, and in 1960 breeding was finally proved. By 1965 there were twelve males singing among the reed beds of Stodmarsh and at the end of the decade breeding was established at Minsmere and another Suffolk coastal site.

By 1975 there were breeding birds in Norfolk and Devon, and in 1978 it was present at fourteen sites, with up to twenty-six breeding pairs. At that time breeding was established in Devon, Dorset, Kent, Norfolk, Nottingham, Suffolk, Warwickshire and two other unnamed counties. Savi's Warbler had come back not because of an increase in habitat nor because of the new-found enlightenment prevalent in Britain, but because population dynamics had allowed it to increase on the Continent and spread outwards to peripheral areas. It is a story not so much of conservation success as of the natural success of a particular species responding to circumstances that we do not yet understand. What is clear, however, is that by the time that Savi's Warbler was ready to spread to Britain the coastal marshes of Suffolk were suitable and waiting.

Thus, what started with the simple, if exciting, return of the Avocet to Suffolk marshes created by wartime emergencies has led to the establishment of Britain's greatest wetland bird reserve. Minsmere, now owned by the RSPB, has been at the centre of this part of our story. There are other, similarly created, wetlands nearby, some of which are nature reserves in their own right. Walberswick is now a National Nature Reserve, Havergate an RSPB reserve, and plans are afoot to take other areas of this bird-rich coast into the conservation fold. Minsmere, however, remains the jewel. It was the first to see breeding Avocets for a hundred years; it cared for Marsh Harriers when they were all but extinct elsewhere; it supported the Bittern in its hour of need and may do so again as that bird continues to decline; it received the expanding population of Bearded Tits just at the right time; and was ready for the recolonizing Savi's Warbler when it returned. All but the Bearded Tit are birds that have come back from extinction in our islands — the debt we owe to the RSPB for its work at Minsmere is difficult to overstate.

Chapter Eight

Back to the Floods

The early history of the Black-tailed Godwit in Britain is certainly lost, and any idea of its former status must of necessity be largely guesswork. Certainly by 1800 it was very much reduced in numbers and local extinction seemed inevitable. It still bred in Norfolk, Cambridgeshire and Lincolnshire, as well as in east Yorkshire, but had already disappeared from Suffolk. Writing in 1838, Jardine says:

> This handsome species breeds annually in the fenny districts of England ... Of old, the Black-tailed Godwit was considered a delicacy for the table, and at present are occasionally taken during or previous to the breeding season, and fatted by the fen men for the London markets; but Mr Yarrell does not consider them to be held in such high estimation for the table as the ruff, when treated in the same manner.

Sir Thomas Browne disagreed, 'the daintiest dish in England' he called it.

Black-tailed Godwits were well known to the fenman, who took them at every opportunity. Eggs were collected for food and the adults, whether breeding or not, were snared or shot. No doubt Godwits had been a favourite, even traditional, quarry, but the eighteenth-century passion for drainage had by 1800 reduced the area of suitable territory to a fraction of what it had been only a hundred years earlier. With drainage the birds simply disappeared and the traditional fenman along with them.

In the restricted areas of marsh that remained the fenman carried on as before, plying his traditional trades and skills, which included plundering the Black-tailed Godwit. But as the birds became rarer and more difficult to obtain, so, according to the simple laws of supply and demand, the price they fetched became higher and higher. By the end of the eighteenth century a fattened Godwit could fetch between 2s 6d and 5s, a fortune by today's standards, and certainly more expensive than, say, smoked salmon or, conceivably, caviar. By this time, however, the bird was so rare that it attracted the attention of collectors of eggs and skins, who quickly polished off the remnant population. Though the headquarters had been the fen districts of Norfolk and Lincolnshire, the existence of a 'Whelpmoor' near Lakenheath clearly indicates that the birds had once bred in Suffolk — 'whelp' or 'yarwhelp' being common country names for both godwits. The last nests were found at Horsey in Norfolk in 1829, the eggs taken and the birds shot by a Mr Rising. By coincidence the same year saw the last birds in Yorkshire, where they formerly nested on Hatfield Moor and in the East Riding. Thereafter the Black-tailed Godwit became only a rather scarce bird of passage on its way to and from its breeding grounds in Holland and Denmark. Just occasionally, however, the odd pair did remain to nest.

At the sale of Mr E.S. Preston's egg collection at Steven's Auction Rooms, lot 95 was a clutch of three Godwits' eggs taken at Reedham in 1857. Possible breeding also occurred in Huntingdonshire and Cambridgeshire in 1847 and in Lincolnshire in 1885. Then in 1914 breeding was suspected in Morayshire in Scotland and birds were noted summering in suitable habitat in Orkney between 1910 and 1914. Though Bannerman 'discounts the suggestion' of breeding in that island group as 'most unlikely', the birds certainly have bred in recent years.

However, in 1934 Jim Vincent, the noted Norfolk watcher, observed a pair at Salthouse and though their behaviour strongly suggested that they had a nest nearby, breeding remained unproven. In 1937 a pair laid eggs in 'southern England' according to Witherby, though the actual location was in East Anglia. The nest was found on 3 May, but no young were reared. On 16 May 1940, Mr W.S. Gunton found a nest with four eggs in south Lincolnshire, where the previous year a pair had also been present. The same site was occupied again in 1941 and the young were photographed.

In 1946 Alan Pilkington discovered and photographed a nest near the north coast of Caithness, the first proven breeding in Scotland. Two young were found. Then in 1948 a pair probably bred on Unst in Shetland. In 1949 Bernard Tucker, of *Handbook* fame, found chicks toward the end of June, but in 1950, despite the presence of two pairs on the island, no chicks were reared. There is some evidence that egg collectors may have been involved, a continuing

Once a popular delicacy, Black-tailed Godwits were specially fattened for the market by Fenland trappers. The birds returned to the Fens in the 1950s and have since spread elsewhere.

menace to any rare bird trying to establish a foothold in Britain. Though absent in 1951 and 1952, Godwits have returned to Unst on and off ever since. In 1957 they were definitely robbed by an egg collector and in 1978 the local observer was able to write 'This site has become too well known and disturbance by bird-watchers may have affected successful breeding.'

In Suffolk, Major G. Aylmer and William H. Payn discovered a pair of Godwits at Lakenheath in July 1947 which, from their behaviour, appeared to have young. A roadman subsequently reported seeing the adults with young, but with great prudence Payn describes the record as 'not proven' in his book *The Birds of Suffolk*.

Then in 1952, at the beginning of May, a local schoolmaster Ted Cottier found a nest with four eggs at Welney on the Ouse Washes.

The fact was a well-kept secret, known only to local observers and the RSPB, and was not made public until 1958, though even then the location and name of the discoverer were withheld. However, by 1958 the RSPB were only acknowledging the already widely-known fact that Godwits were breeding regularly on the Ouse Washes. The Washes were created as a safety valve when the Dutchman Cornelius Vermuyden started draining this area of the fens on behalf of the Earl of Bedford in 1630. By straightening and embanking the rivers, huge areas of marsh were drained and converted to rich agricultural land. Winter, however, frequently brought more water than the rivers could cope with and, rather than be allowed to flood the whole area indiscriminately, the surplus was channelled into the Washes. Between Earith in the south and Denver in the north stretch two twenty-mile-long embankments almost a mile apart. The area between the two forms the Washes. In some winters the whole may be extensively flooded, in others there may be very little water indeed. It is interesting to note that it is the area around Welney that always floods first and that Black-tailed Godwits invariably nest among grassland subject to winter floods.

So, in the summer of 1952, a pair of Godwits had nested, but optimism at the RSPB headquarters was short-lived. On 22 May the discoverer Ted Cottier found that Carrion Crows had stolen the clutch and the birds had disappeared. It was a local cowman who rediscovered them a couple of miles away and on 22 July Ted Cottier found the replacement nest and three youngsters just able to fly.

The spring of 1953 saw three pairs established on the Washes, but Carrion Crows were an ever-present threat, and the chances of the grazing cows that inhabited the fields in summer accidentally trampling a nest were always high. In the event only one nest, thoughtfully protected by a wire fence erected by two local herdsmen, hatched young. Others, including replacements, were robbed by Crows and one was trampled. In the following year, 1954, once again three pairs nested, this time with more success, and two broods were reared. But by now the secret was out and many local bird-watchers were well aware of what was happening. Nevertheless, a remarkable amount of restraint was shown and the Godwit population gradually built up until 1961, when eleven pairs all hatched young. There may well have been more, for birds were certainly present in other parts of the area, though their nests were not found. The following table documents the first ten years of breeding on the Washes.

Year	Number of Pairs	Number of Nests (including replacements)	Number of Broods
1952	1	2	1
1953	3	4	1
1954	3	3	2
1955	4	6	4
1956	7	9	3
1957	6	7	6
1958	9	9	9
1959	12	12	10
1960	12	12	12
1961	11	11	11

This build-up was not without event. In 1955 many nests were washed out by floods, though the birds laid again and reared young. Nevertheless, Crows remained a menace and it was not until 1957, the first year that the number of pairs had actually fallen since the recolonization began, that an all-out war was started. In that season no less than 180 Crows' eggs were destroyed by an agile local bird-watcher. By continuing the pressure the threat has diminished and the number of successful Godwit nests has increased accordingly.

By 1977 no less than fifty-two pairs could be found breeding on the Ouse Washes, mostly with success. The Black-tailed Godwit had returned. Along the way, and for differing reasons and purposes, much of the Washes had been acquired by conservation bodies as nature reserves. The RSPB started acquiring land in 1964 near Welches Dam and erected public hides from which birds can be watched free of charge. Today the RSPB owns or leases 628 acres. The Cambridge and Isle of Ely Naturalists' Trust started buying in 1965 and now has a reserve of 305 acres and the Wildfowl Trust has a reserve at Welney of 619 acres. Between them these conservation bodies are now by far the largest landowners in the Washes and have a significant say in the running of the whole area.

Gradually Black-tailed Godwits have colonized other areas of

Britain, and though the Ouse Washes remain the primary site it is hoped that this outward trend will continue. By 1978 there were two pairs in Cambridgeshire, eight pairs in Norfolk, three in Suffolk, four in Somerset, one in Shetland, and perhaps as many as eight other pairs in two other counties. The previous year they had also bred in Cumbria, Kent and Orkney. The outlook for the future of the Black-tailed Godwit in Britain is distinctly rosy.

There is little doubt that the first colonists had their origins in Holland, where a huge population exists. Though a decidedly scarce visitor after its demise as a British breeder in the early part of the nineteenth century, the frequency of occurrence of the Godwit both as a passage migrant and winter visitor increased remarkably prior to the 1952 recolonization. From 1923 to 1937 less than 2,000 birds were noted; whereas from 1938 to 1952 the total was over 41,000. In Suffolk, to take a single county as an example, the largest flock prior to 1930 was thirteen birds; whereas by the late 1950s flocks of 400 to 500 were comparatively common. Along with this startling increase in numbers there was also an increase in the number of birds summering in East Anglia.

The Ouse Washes, already the primary home of the Black-tailed Godwit, were soon to see two more former breeders re-establishing themselves in Britain — the Ruff and the Black Tern. Ruffs were once abundant in England and highly favoured as a delicacy in medieval times. There are records of banquets at which hundreds of Ruffs were served, including one at Cawood in Yorkshire in 1466 quoted by Bannerman where 'of the fowles called Rees there were supplied 200 dozen'. Writing in 1789, Pennant mentioned that fattened Ruffs cost 2s to 2s6d each, while twenty years later Montagu put the price at 30s to 42s a dozen. He also added that the 'fattener' paid no more than 10s a dozen to the fenmen who captured the birds with snares and clap nets set on their traditional lekking grounds. Ruffs evidently travelled well and the traders undertook lengthy journeys to dispose of their wares, after fattening them on a diet of wheat, bread and milk mixed with hempseed and sugar. The eggs were also considered a delicacy. It was, however, the drainage of the fens, so damaging to the Black-tailed Godwit, that also put paid to the Ruff. By 1865 Ruffs had disap-

A female Ruff, or Reeve as it should be known. Once again Reeves can be found at their nests in parts of East Anglia and perhaps elsewhere in the marshy districts of England.

peared from their former haunts in Durham, Yorkshire, Huntingdonshire, Cambridgeshire, Northamptonshire, Suffolk and Somerset and remained only in Norfolk and possibly Lincolnshire. By then commercial snaring had become uneconomic and the residual population had claimed the attention of the specimen and egg collector. Two pairs returned to Norfolk in 1871 only to have, as one writer put it, 'their whole progeny shot'. There were no records for the next few years until a bird was found with eggs at Hickling in 1878. Another nest was found at the same site in 1884 and every subsequent year until 1890. Thereafter the last toehold of the Ruff in Britain was abandoned.

Just occasionally the odd Ruff bred in Britain as, for instance, in 1898 on the Duke of Grafton's estate in Suffolk. In 1902 two nests were discovered next to the Tees in County Durham. The birds returned the following year but no nests were found. In 1907 attempted breeding took place in Norfolk and the Reeve was photographed at the nest by Miss E.L. Turner. The eggs failed to hatch. On 20 April 1910 a clutch of eggs was taken at Southport, Lancashire, though the adult bird was not seen. In 1922 A.W. Boyd found a nest at Cley in Norfolk, the last for over forty years.

Thereafter the Ruff remained only a regular bird of passage; a scarce but increasing winter visitor, and a non-breeding summer visitor to previously favoured haunts such as the north Norfolk coast. Then, after several years of suspicion, breeding was proved at the Ouse Washes in 1963. A single nest the following year was followed by two nests in 1965 and 1966. None were found in 1967, but two in 1968 were followed by five in 1969, no less than ten in 1970, and twenty-one in 1971.

In general Reeves' nests are not easily found, especially by those wishing to cause as little disturbance as possible to a bird trying to re-establish itself. Reeves are also invariably outnumbered by the Ruffs who, having mated promiscuously, take no further interest in the breeding routine. Thus the twenty-one nests of 1971 were built by Reeves in attendance at leks where a total of 103 Ruffs had gathered.

By 1971 birds had bred in North Wales, Lancashire, and Lincolnshire, and seemed likely to have done so in Essex and Kent. Thus the 1970s opened with an air of optimism for the future of the Ruff in Britain. Yet, as is so often the way, this optimism was to be severely tried in subsequent years. In 1978 only three sites were occupied: a single Reeve appeared at an old breeding site in Cambridgeshire; four Ruffs and three Reeves were recorded at a Lancashire lek but breeding was not proved; and the Ouse Washes' leks were washed out by flooding. Yet in 1979 there were more sites occupied than ever before and, with twenty-one Reeves breeding, it was one of the best years ever. More recent information is less precise, but there is some evidence of a strong lek in Norfolk, though clearly great care must be taken in making assumptions when discussing the safety, or otherwise, of colonizing birds.

Within a couple of years watchers at the Ouse Washes had yet another cause for celebration. In 1966 they were able to count about twenty-five pairs of Black-tailed Godwits, two nesting Reeves, and the first Black Terns to breed in Britain since 1858. Certainly the area must have seemed more like a Dutch polder than a part of England.

Even as late as the early nineteenth century Black Terns bred among the Fens and in Broadland in large numbers. Rivière writes that they 'bred in thousands', and earlier Thomas Pennant described the scene at East Fen in 1769: 'Black Terns abound . . . in vast flocks [that] almost deafen one with their clamors.' Certainly it bred at Upton ('myriads' in 1818), Horsey, Winterton and Crowland Wash ('great numbers' 1832) and it seems strange that it did not continue to do so. The drainage of the fens certainly eliminated one of the major strongholds, but the Broadland area remained more or less as it always had. Persecution no doubt played a part, for egg and skin collectors certainly took their toll, but the final demise remains a mystery.

Nesting took place in 1853, when much of the Fen district was flooded and three clutches were certainly taken from Feltwell Fen. Then a clutch of two eggs and the two adult birds were taken at Sutton in 1858 — the last nesting attempt of the century.

Only one other area held breeding Black Terns — Romney Marsh in Kent. But here too they were fast declining and by 1837 were, according to Yarrell, decidedly rare. By the middle or late 1840s the Black Tern ceased to breed in Britain completely.

From 1858 to 1941 the Black Tern was no more than a spring and autumn passage migrant in variable numbers, mainly through southern England, but occasionally extending northwards to Yorkshire. Then there took place one of those strange quirks of ornithology that Britain seems so prone to. Just as the marshes of Minsmere and other areas of the Suffolk coast were flooded as a part of wartime defences against possible German invasion, so were several areas of the south coast, including a thousand acres between the old

The Black Tern at a platform nest. Though it has bred on several occasions in recent years, this graceful bird has yet to secure a regular place as a British breeding bird.

Cinque Port of Winchelsea and the sea, known as Pett Level. A Mr R. Cooke, who had special duties and thus had privileged access to the area (presumably the same R. Cooke who discovered the Black Redstarts of 1909) discovered no less than eight pairs of Black Terns nesting on an island of driftwood and detritus on 10 June 1941. Each had three eggs and by mid-August there were twenty-three birds present, including fledged young. Fortunately for the birds the area was occupied by the military authorities and remained undisturbed. In 1942 five pairs returned to breed, again rearing young. In 1943 birds returned, but the island had been taken over by Black-headed Gulls and the Black Terns moved away. By 1944, the threat of invasion being past, Pett Level was once again dry and unsuitable for the Terns. So, it seemed, Black Terns were quite able to recolonize Britain should suitable conditions become available.

On the face of it the Pett Level story seems perfectly reasonable, but by the time that the British Ornithologists' Union (BOU) produced their *Status of Birds in Britain and Ireland* in 1971 the Pett Level occurrences were dismissed with 'the supposed breeding in Sussex in 1941 and 1942 is now discounted'.

It was not until 1966 that Black Terns finally nested once again in Britain. In the summer of that year several pairs were present and found to be building nests on the Ouse Washes; two pairs laid eggs and three young flew. All looked set for the Ouse Washes to see the return of yet another lost bird — but it was not to be. In 1967 the birds did not return to the Washes, though by a strange twist of fate a pair chose that year to nest in Ireland for the first time, rearing a single chick on an island in a lough. The following year was again a blank at the Ouse Washes, but in 1969 six pairs nested, though only a single youngster flew. In 1970 a single pair nested elsewhere in East Anglia, but in the years from 1971 to 1974 no Black Terns bred anywhere in Britain. Then in 1975 there were pairs in England and in Ireland. The years 1976 and 1977 were blank, but once again the birds returned in 1978. On this occasion they settled and laid eggs on a Nottinghamshire flood, but were robbed by an egg collector who substituted stones for the eggs.

Whether or not the Black Tern can be classed as a recolonist on the evidence of such erratic breeding is open to interpretation. Clearly it will now nest with us if conditions are suitable, but it has not yet settled down to breed on a regular basis, despite the efforts made by conservation bodies at the Ouse Washes. If it is to form a permanent colony it would seem most likely to be in this area. The Ouse Washes are one of Britain's most important wetlands and it is reassuring to know that so much of the area is in the hands of various conservation bodies. In winter they are home to one of the greatest concentrations of wildfowl in western Europe and now, in summer, they have these unique breeding birds, at least three of which have returned to Britain after lengthy absences.

Chapter Nine

A Star is Born

In the spring of 1954 a pair of Ospreys built a nest at a secret site among the lakes and forests of Speyside. They shared their home with Crested Tits, Crossbills and Capercaillies and hunted the local lochs for trout and pike. Though they were seen by bird-watchers, who speculated about their breeding for the first time in Britain for over forty years, their whereabouts remained a secret. Then in July the son of local RSPB warden, Desmond Nethersole-Thompson, discovered the nest. Eventually two young Ospreys flew. These, or other birds, may have nested in 1953 but the early history of the return of the Osprey to Britain remains shrouded in mystery, despite the fact that at three feet deep and five feet across the Osprey builds one of the largest nests in the world.

A pair returned to the same eyrie early the following year. They settled down, repaired their old nest and the hen laid her eggs. There then appeared on the scene one of the Osprey's oldest enemies — the egg collector. The clutch was stolen; the blown eggs now presumably lie in a bed of cotton wool in some old cabinet somewhere in Britain. The birds moved on and settled in a small, half-dead pine overlooking Loch Garten, where they constructed another nest, perhaps on the basis of one they had used in a previous season. Certainly it was a huge structure and, though it had not been discovered by bird-watchers, it had not escaped the notice of egg collectors. Here too the hen laid a clutch of eggs and here too they were taken.

Persistent to the end, the birds then moved high up the Spey to the Sluggan Pass, where they began a third nest in a dead pine. Here in June they were discovered by Mr Huntley, a bird-watcher from Newcastle, who was holidaying among the ornithological delights of this bird-rich valley. The thrill of discovery cannot be described, for this was the first fully authenticated Osprey nest since the First World War, but it was too late in the season and the birds soon drifted away. Later the deserted Loch Garten nest was discovered.

The history of the demise of the original Scottish Ospreys is a depressing story. Harried virtually without respite for a century or more there remained by 1850 only two major strongholds — Speyside and Sutherland. The final extinction of the bird in these two areas is largely the story of two brothers, Lewis and William Dunbar, and the two collectors with whom they worked. The brothers came from Bonar Bridge and were quite straightforwardly in it for the money. They collected eggs and specimens to supply their rich English customers and were intrepid in pursuit of their quarry. William first visited Sutherland in 1847, by which time the Osprey population had already been decimated by the establishment of shooting interests following the Highland 'clearances' of 1807 and onwards. Virtually single-handed he eliminated the population — the last pair nested in 1850. Meanwhile his brother Lewis had made a speciality of the Speyside area and the celebrated Loch an Eilean in particular. Year after year he robbed these birds, pursuing them even to their replacement nests. It is arguable that the Dunbar brothers wreaked the biggest ornitho-disaster in individual terms in the history of British birds.

Having robbed the eyrie and shot the female on Loch an Laig Aird in 1847, William was engaged as guide by Charles William George St John to accompany him on a tour of Sutherland in 1848. A full account of this trip can be found in his *Natural History and Sport in Moray* published posthumously from his notes and letters in 1863. St John, despite the bad press he has enjoyed during the current conservation-conscious era, was undoubtedly a fine naturalist. He made many valuable observations and recorded accurately and in detail; indeed it is the very detail of his writing that makes his work so valuable as a source of damning quotes. One quote in particular has been overworked by conservationists ever since. Indeed it could not have been better written.

> I lamented the absence of the birds. Why the poor Osprey should be so persecuted I know not, as it is quite harmless, living wholly on fish, of which everyone knows there is too great an abundance in this country for the most rigid preserver to grudge this picturesque bird his share.

Written by one of the final exterminators of the Scottish Osprey these are crocodile tears indeed. Undoubtedly St John was typical of his time — a time when natural history and sport (i.e. shooting) were totally complementary. The good sportsman, even today, knows a great deal more than the average conservationist would care to credit him with.

St John was, then, primarily a sportsman and naturalist, not an egg or skin collector. He did, however, have a number of friends, notably Mr Hancock of Newcastle, who were collectors and he was not averse to keeping the odd specimen for himself. The taking of a Crossbill nest gave him great joy: 'At last I have them safe, four beautiful eggs like a greenfinch's, longer in the shape, the nest also with the branch. I fear the old birds have travelled too much to skin well; they are a green one and a red one ... I consider it a great victory.' He was also a keen falconer and raided Peregrine eyries to acquire young birds for training.

Setting out, then, with William Dunbar he got straight into his stride on 23 May 1848. At Loch an Laig Aird near Scourie they found an occupied Osprey's eyrie on an island in a loch, the classic site of the original Scottish birds. The recent colonists are invariably tree nesters. 'I must say' he writes 'that I would rather she had escaped this fate; but as her skin was wanted, I agreed to try to kill her ... at last I fired, and the poor bird, after wheeling about for a few moments, fell far to leeward of me, and down in the most precipitous and rocky part of the mountain.' Though he does not say so, the bird was not recovered. The duo then rowed over to collect the 'two beautiful eggs' and 'as we came away, we still observed the male bird unceasingly calling and seeking for his hen. I was really sorry that I had shot her.'

Moving quickly onwards St John and Dunbar found themselves at another Osprey eyrie at Loch na Claise Carnaich near Rhiconnich on 12 June. 'As my gun was loaded' after a difficult stalk over broken ground had brought him within forty yards of the male 'I knew he could scarcely escape; so standing up, I took a good look at him, expecting that he would see me and fly ... whether from the earnestness with which he was watching Dunbar (who was busily swimming out to collect eggs and young from the island eyrie) or from the manner in which his head-feathers projected, he did not see me at all. After waiting a short time without his moving, I am sorry to say that I shot him deliberately in cold blood as he sat.'

These passages show not only the strange sense of fairness shared

Years of rumour, secrecy, intrigue and argument marked the return of the Osprey to Scotland after an absence of fifty years. Now its return is announced on television every year.

by 'sportsmen' to the present day at not shooting the sitting bird, but also the extraordinary innocence of St John. Pangs of guilt, yes, but insufficiently strong for him not to wish to boast to his friends of his conquests.

After this he and Dunbar returned to the original site 'Where . . . in May I shot the old hen, taking at the same time two eggs. Mr Dunbar, with his usual perseverance went to the nest . . . and found that the male bird had got another mate, and that she was . . . sitting on a single egg.' Naturally enough Dunbar secured that one as well. The same day he also swam out to the eyrie at Loch an Iasgair, but found the nest empty for the second time that season. So, at the end of their tour of destruction the dreadful duo had shot three adults and taken four young and four eggs of the Osprey.

The following year, 1849, it was John Wolley's turn at the

Sutherland Ospreys. The 5 May saw him at Loch na Claise Carnaich, where St John had bagged the male as he perched the
previous year. He swam out to the eyrie and collected three eggs,
though not without a great deal of suffering *en route*. Moving on
to the Loch an Laig Aird he was disappointed to find it deserted.

Meanwhile Lewis Dunbar, William's brother, had sent three
eggs taken at Loch Morlich on Speyside to Charles St John who
passed one on to Mr Hancock in Newcastle. On 24 May, for the
second successive year, he raided the Loch an Eilean eyrie and sent
the three eggs direct to Hancock. In 1850 he sent yet another clutch
of three to Hancock, who, by now presumably amassing one of the
greatest collections of British Ospreys' eggs, decided to visit Scotland on his own account. Together with Lewis Dunbar he visited
the Loch Morlich site, where Ospreys regularly nested on the ruins
of a burnt-out shooting lodge. Two eggs were found in the nest and
Dunbar was placed in ambush to shoot the female as she returned
to the nest. On skinning the bird Hancock discovered a third egg
ready to lay to add to the other two Dunbar collected.

In 1851 Lewis Dunbar once again took two eggs from Loch an
Eilean, on this occasion swimming ashore on his back with one egg
in each hand. These were sent to John Wolley, as were the three that
Dunbar took on his final raid in 1852. By good fortune Lewis
Dunbar emigrated to Australia in 1853, but by then it was already
too late for the Scottish Ospreys. Brother William had already
written to John Wolley in June 1850 'I believe at this moment, there
is only one osprey's nest in this country . . . I am afraid that Mr St
John, yourself and your humble servant have finally done for the
ospreys.'

On and off for the next fifty years the Ospreys persevered with
their attempts at breeding at Loch an Eilean, or in nearby
Rothiemurchus. Mostly they were robbed by egg collectors, but
sometimes youngsters were reared. Right at the end of the century,
for the four years 1894 to 1897, the Loch an Eilean site produced
young, and the efforts of J.P. Grant, Laird of Rothiemurchus, who
had protected the birds in the late 1880s and early 1890s, seemed to
have been successful. Then they missed 1898; nested but failed in
1899; and though they visited Loch an Eilean they never nested
again.

Elsewhere in Inverness the last two pairs continued breeding into the twentieth century. At Loch Arkaig a pair nested regularly on an island, in an old oak protected by the Laird, Donald Cameron of Lochiel. 'In 1908' Cameron wrote 'the nest was placed under police protection, the tree was encircled with barbed wire, and a sunk barbed wire fence was put round the island, but all to little avail.' The birds nested successfully that year, but thereafter only a solitary individual returned until it too disappeared in 1913. The last Scottish Ospreys continued to nest on an island in Loch Loyne until 1916, but then they too disappeared. So a healthy population of a magnificent bird had been eliminated in a little over a hundred years. It was to be another forty before the first colonists were to return.

Accounts of how Ospreys returned to breed in Speyside are never more than approximations of the truth. Despite their size and obviousness, the early history of their return remains a mystery. From time to time during the early 1950s bird-watchers watched these magnificent birds as they plunged feet first into hill lochs in their search for cruising trout and pike. Some even watched the birds carrying their prey away into the forest, yet their nests remained the subject of speculation rather than fact. Even the breeding in 1954, reported by Nethersole-Thompson's son, retains an element of doubt in some ornithological circles. Only in 1955 was the first fully authenticated nest found.

Working on the basis of a probable re-use of the same eyrie, the RSPB anticipated a return to the Sluggan Pass in 1956 and began preparations for their reception. Large and obvious birds like the Osprey could hardly, they argued, be overlooked. Bird-watchers would want to see them and egg collectors would seek them out too. Both guarding and viewing operations would be needed if success was to be assured. Enlisting the enthusiastic help of the local landowner, Colonel J.P. Grant, an observation post was built overlooking the Sluggan nest.

All was in vain; in 1956 the birds did not return but found instead the forest of Rothiemurchus more to their liking. Here they settled down, unbeknown to the RSPB, and were discovered by Desmond Nethersole-Thompson's daughter, close to the family home. In late May or early June the nest was robbed, probably by a Crow, possibly with the assistance of an over-zealous bird-watcher. The causes of the disaster remain a mystery and the subject of considerable acrimony. Indeed the accounts of these early seasons have been written up by those concerned with such venom that it is difficult to find even the bare facts. In his 'official' RSPB account of the Osprey's return (*The Return of the Osprey* by Philip Brown and George Waterston), Philip Brown criticizes Nethersole-Thompson for his secrecy and the disturbance caused by tape-recording the birds at this 1956 eyrie. Well guarded and watched over, he implies, this nest would have stood a better chance of success. As we lack the facts behind the disaster we are in no position to judge the case. What is certain is that the Ospreys do not belong to the RSPB, to the government, the Crown, the landowner, the discoverer, or to anyone else. Anyone involved in conservation is entitled to his or her own view about what course of action to follow when a rare breeding bird is discovered — secrecy or publicity, both have their advantages and both their adherents. Personally I favour publicity, as does the RSPB in many cases. But, if I may digress briefly, I once discovered a breeding colony of the extremely elusive and decidedly rare Spotted Crake in suburban Surrey one June evening. I immediately telephoned an official of the local natural history society (then or later also a member of the RSPB Council). The following evening the area was inundated by bird-watchers, some of whom had to 'see' the birds for their 'life lists' and tramped across the fields to flush them. Secrecy, then, may have its place after all!

So the Rothiemurchus nest of 1956 met with disaster. Once more the birds moved on, this time to Loch Morlich, where they again started to build a replacement nest. But as at Sluggan in the previous year, the attempt was half-hearted and the pair abandoned the idea and drifted away. In 1957 the RSPB used every effort to locate and protect the birds. They borrowed a cottage in Rothiemurchus, but no birds showed up. They hired a caravan when a bird appeared at Loch Garten, and their watchers had a frustrated spring watching a single Osprey go desultorily through the business of repairing a nest that was not to be used.

In 1958 a pair of Ospreys finally settled down at the Loch Garten eyrie, though not until early May and after giving their RSPB would-be godparents the most heart-breaking April. Immediately code-worded telegrams flashed across the country with military precision, if fewer resources. 'Operation Inflation' was put into full swing. An observation post was established a quarter of a mile from the tree and plans were made to move closer once the eggs had been laid. Meanwhile a team of observers would work round-the-clock shifts to prevent casual bird-watchers disturbing the Ospreys. Philip Brown, Bob Dawkins and George Waterston were all on hand, and debate about the best methods of protecting the birds occupied many a long hour. Eventually, as is the way with such affairs, a compromise was reached. The base camp would remain a quarter of a mile from the nest. A forward watch-out, used in a previous year, was established two hundred yards from the eyrie, backed up by a sleeping tent a further fifty yards away, the two connected by a pull cord for signalling. Despite a visit by a one-time egg collector, who shinned up the tree and caused no end of disturbance to the Ospreys, the eyrie remained physically unprotected.

It was Philip Brown who found himself on forward duty, peering through binoculars on the fateful night of 2/3 June. At 2.25 a.m., just as the first glimmerings of the new day began to make it possible to see, the sitting Osprey flew up screaming. Brown pulled the cord to awaken Bert Axell, then on a busman's holiday from his wardenship of Dungeness. Together they rushed over the squelchy two hundred yards that separated the forward watch-out from the tree, up which they could see a climber, virtually at the nest. Shouting and blowing whistles as they ran, Brown and Axell disturbed the intruder as he reached the nest. He made his escape in the dark leaving behind a smashed Osprey egg at the foot of the tree. The nest was examined and found to contain two eggs. Only later in the day, when the unusual behaviour of the hen alerted attention, was it decided to chance further disturbance and check out the nest in the full light of day. A second smashed Osprey egg, like the first containing a partially developed embryo, was discovered at the foot of the tree and the two eggs in the nest turned out to be hens' eggs smeared with boot polish.

The deprived birds, doubtless disillusioned with their original nest, started once again building a new nest in an electricity pylon and then, more sensibly, in another Scot's Pine near the Loch. By the end of June they had given up and moved away. So all the plans and efforts had been in vain; or had they?

The year 1959 was to be the first year, debatable 1954 apart, that young Ospreys had been reared in Britain since the early part of the century, though Waterston and Brown did not know it as they planned their campaign. The Loch Garten area was declared a bird reserve; the nesting tree was lopped of its easily climbable limbs and both it and the replacement nest tree were swathed in barbed wire; a new forward hide that could accommodate two watchers in some degree of comfort was built near the original eyrie; duck-boards were laid across the marsh reducing the 'running time' to the tree substantially; and the 'communication cord' was replaced by a field telephone. There was to be no repeat of the 1958 fiasco.

The birds returned on 18 to 22 April and immediately began building up the previous year's replacement eyrie. All the boards, the forward hide and the telephone had to be ripped up and repositioned under cloak of darkness. Early in June the chicks hatched and the RSPB, apparently mainly George Waterston, decided to break the news to the media and make preparations for visitors to view the Ospreys from a well-positioned hide. Suddenly the birds were news and no less than 14,000 visitors were admitted free to see them. This was the start of the most extraordinary piece of ornitho-public relations ever seen in Britain, or elsewhere come to that. The same nest was viewed by no less than 55,000 people in the first three successful years, during which the AA erected road signs and the RSPB staff became ushers and usherettes rather than wardens. It was during this period that bird-watchers told (probably apocryphal) stories about overhearing tourists saying 'Have you seen the Ostriches?' Over the years, and at the time of writing the birds are celebrating their twenty-first anniversary, the Ospreys of Loch Garten have been seen by almost a million people including most of the royal family and no less than three prime ministers — all free of charge. There are now displays and commentaries, souvenirs and sometimes a glimpse of the birds at the nest through powerful binoculars trained on them. The camp is now permanent, the staff well organized, the birds safe (though some strangely demented vandal sawed half-way through the nesting tree one winter) and the RSPB gains at least five hundred new members every year. The visitor to Speyside, now one of our primary holiday areas, is bound to include Loch Garten in his itinerary even if he knows nothing at all about birds.

Slowly Ospreys began to colonize other parts of Scotland. In

Wings up, pinions spread, an Osprey brakes to land at its nest.
From a single pair in the late 1950s it has built up a healthy
population north of the border.

1963 a second pair laid eggs and in 1964 a third pair was present. By
1978 no less than twenty-two pairs were present making some
attempt at breeding. Eleven pairs were successful, rearing nineteen
or twenty young between them. In 1979 twenty-five or twenty-six
pairs reared no less than thirty to thirty-three young — the most
successful season to date. The menace of the egg collector still
looms large on the scene, however. In 1977, for example, the first
pair of Ospreys to lay a clutch of four eggs this century was robbed
by collectors. So it is perhaps not surprising that the location of
only one other pair has been made public — at Loch of Lowes in
Perthshire, a reserve of the Scottish Naturalists' Trust. Despite the
spread, and by 1971 there were at least seven distinct sites, that year
saw the Loch Garten nest robbed once again by an egg collector
who overcame all the precautions and the twenty-four-hour man-

ning of the RSPB. Whether the British-taken eggs of an Osprey are worth the effort and risk involved, or whether it is the challenge of the Loch Garten eyrie is unknown. What is clear is that if the RSPB had not acted so quickly and effectively the Osprey population would not be in the healthy state that it is today. The robbers of 1971 were fined a paltry £50, the maximum the law of the time allowed.

There can be no doubt that the Scottish Ospreys are an overspill from the Scandinavian colony and, according to Leslie Brown, an influx of immigrants probably continues to augment the population. In Sweden, the probable area of origin of our birds, the Osprey was persecuted until it was given protection in the 1920s. Thereafter it increased rapidly and, despite increasing evidence of mercury and other poisons, reached a population of about 1,000 pairs in 1970. A result of this increase was a spread in the late 1940s and 1950s into Norway, a country which could boast of no more than three or four pairs in the 1930s. By 1956 twenty-seven pairs were known and numbers were increasing. In Finland too there is evidence of an increase from a very small population in the 1920s to between 500 and 1,000 pairs in the 1960s. It is interesting to speculate that this upsurge of the Scandinavian population owes something to the respite provided by the Second World War, but as Sweden remained neutral and more or less 'normal' it would be sheer presumption to put the increase down to this cause. Protection seems a much more likely explanation. Today the European population is estimated at 12,000 birds, of which about 1,000 are shot each year, mainly on migration.

The Osprey now seems well established in Britain once again. Doubtless pairs will continue to be robbed by egg collectors and some will be disturbed by bird-watchers, but the pressure on the individual pair is now much less intense than in the early days of recolonization. With luck the Osprey will spread back over its former Scottish range and perhaps even return to breed in England once again.

Though the return of the Osprey to Scotland can clearly be attributed to the species' increasing numbers in Scandinavia, the changed attitude towards wildlife in Britain is certainly also a contributory factor. If a pair had returned between the two wars there can be little doubt that both they and their eggs would have ended up in collectors' cases. This new awareness of, and care for wildlife and the countryside has been detailed and explained elsewhere in this book, but the Ospreys themselves, via the RSPB, have been a significant factor in extending this awareness. By coincidence the Ospreys chose a period during which the human population was becoming more mobile and seeking more leisure time in the countryside. The Aviemore Centre, with its rash of hotels and ski facilities, is but a symptom of this growing demand for leisure. Skiing, climbing, walking and pony trekking are all experiencing an amazing boom in popularity and taking more and more people into the hills. Angling too is experiencing the same boom and, with over three million adherents, is reckoned to be the most popular of all British sports. In Scotland the pressure on rivers and lochs has pushed the price of salmon fishing higher and higher. Such pressures have created a simple over-fishing situation that has resulted in a 'put and take' policy in many waters — indeed most waters in southern England. Even in Scotland, however, the need to augment the natural population of trout by regular stocking has led to the growth of numerous fish farms. In artificial stew ponds trout are reared and brought on by regular feeding in comparatively cramped conditions, in what might well prove to be the only 'Osprey Bird Table' in the world. Add in sales of fish to visitors and the whole enterprise sounds so financially appealing that the surprise is that no one is yet attempting it.

Chapter Ten

The Colonizers —the South

Nature is never static. The idea, perpetuated among schoolchildren and by popular journalists, that there is something called 'the balance of nature' that should not be interfered with, may have useful implications for conservation but is totally erroneous. Nature, including populations of animals and plants, is dynamic. Leave a heathland alone and it will, over a century or two, become an oak forest. Along the way its population of plants, birds and mammals will change dramatically. Natural disasters such as fire or volcanic eruption may destroy huge areas of natural vegetation and the animals and plants that inhabit it. Yet soon afterwards recolonization will begin quite naturally. The activities of man on the environment can be regarded as a series of natural disasters, yet when one form of life is eliminated another will quickly take its place. Change, then, is an intrinsic part of the dynamic of nature.

At one time, albeit several hundred thousand years ago, Britain was home to an albatross and a giant tropicbird. More recently the Eagle Owl, Hazel Grouse, Crane and Dalmatian Pelican all bred with us. Gradually as conditions changed they disappeared, their places doubtless taken by other species better able to cope with the new conditions. Even in what seems like the settled conditions of today some birds are declining while others are increasing. These early changes may have taken place over hundreds or thousands of years. Today the pace of change has accelerated. Today it is the actions of people that have the most important effect on evolution. We turn forest into grassland, heaths into arable, we build cities and towns where there were none before, we create waters and dump

1
2

1 Resplendent in summer finery, the Black Tern is one of the most elegant and beautiful of our birds, yet at one time hunting forced the species from the marshes of East Anglia.
2 Most famous of all the birds that have returned after a lengthy absence, the Osprey makes the news every year when it returns to Britain's best-known bird nest at Loch Garten.

waste, indeed we change every aspect of the land and much of the sea. Some birds have declined as a result; others, quick to learn, have taken advantage of man's ways to exploit a new food source and prosper. But lest all changes are put down to man, let me stress once again that even in an apparently settled environment animal populations will naturally change.

As we have seen, several birds have suffered serious declines and some have actually been lost to Britain over the past two hundred years. Some of these have returned and their stories form the backbone of this book. But others have colonized Britain for the first time as far as we know, and it is these that form the subject of this chapter and the next.

Lying on the north-western edge of a large continent Britain draws its birds mainly from the south, east and north. To the west the Atlantic forms an effective barrier to colonization to all but seabirds, though the increasing frequency of some trans-Atlantic vagrants and the startling breeding record of American Spotted Sandpipers in 1975 shows that even the West may produce the occasional colonist. It is, however, to the Continent in the south and to Scandinavia in the north that we must, in the main, look for colonists. In the present century no less than eight species have spread from the south to claim a place in Britain for the first time. First to arrive were Black Redstart and Little Ringed Plover: they were followed by Collared Dove, Firecrest, Mediterranean Gull, Cetti's Warbler, Serin and Little Gull in approximately that order. These birds are to be distinguished from a motley band of species that have bred in Britain erratically, though some are as yet so recently arrived that their occurrences may ultimately prove to be no more than erratic. Only time will tell.

*   *   *

1

2

1 Firecrests have bred in Britain for over twenty years, yet their status remains erratic. Even in the early 1980s there is doubt that they will survive as British breeding birds.
2 To find a pair of Bee-eaters breeding in Britain is an ornithologist's dream. Yet on two quite separate occasions these summer visitors to southern Europe have thrilled their British finders.

Starting, then, at the beginning, the Black Redstart first colonized Britain in 1923, though it did breed as early as 1845 in Durham and 1909 in Sussex. Breeding was first proved in 1923 when a pair was found along the cliffs between Hastings and Fairlight Cove in Sussex by S.D. Herington. This or another pair was present again in 1924. R. Cooke also found a nest in 1923 some four miles to the west at Pett Level, and it was this observer who had noted breeding in an old shepherd's hut at the same place in 1909.

Like most colonizations the birds were at first somewhat erratic. There were regular records in Cornwall in the mid-1920s, and in 1926 the species first appeared in London at the site used for the 1925 Wembley Exhibition. The use of derelict sites in cities was to mark the main colonization of Britain by this species. From 1926 to 1942 the Wembley site housed up to four pairs, the main concentration in the country. Elsewhere it nested at Westminster Abbey in 1940 and 1941, and in 1942 a pair bred at Fenchurch Street: there were more than twenty males singing in London, including one, appropriately, on the Natural History Museum in South Kensington. It was, however, the availability of bombed sites in the City that enabled the Black Redstart to establish itself in Britain. By the end of the war the bird was well established both in London and in Dover, and with inevitable ups and downs the spread has continued to the present day. In 1949, for example, eleven pairs were located in the City, at Cripplegate (five pairs), Ropemaker Street (one), Cannon Street (two), Walbrook (one), Paternoster Row (one) and Billiter Square (one). Between them they produced nineteen broods from which seventy-six young flew. The same year also saw pairs at West Brompton Cemetery and Croydon Power Station, both within the London area.

In the early 1960s the redevelopment of the City was under way and the once flourishing colony was deserted. However, birds turned up on other derelict sites in London, as well as in old railway marshalling yards and other industrial sites such as power stations and gas works. These areas remain their present London base. Elsewhere Black Redstarts are still established at Hastings and other Sussex cliffs, at Dover and the cliffs of east Kent, along the Suffolk coast at Lowestoft, in various parts of the Midlands and as far north as Flamborough Head in Yorkshire, and even Orkney in 1973.

The population varies, or at least appears to vary, considerably

*A female Black Redstart brings food to her eager chicks.
Colonization by this continental bird began in the 1920s, but only
really took off during the Second World War.*

from year to year. Old sites become unsuitable or are redeveloped
and the displaced birds may be missed for a year or two until the
new site is discovered by bird-watchers. However, it seems that a
steady average of about thirty pairs breed most years, with less than
a hundred pairs even in the better years. By 1977 the total was sixty
breeding pairs plus a further forty territory-holding males that may
have bred.

Prior to 1938 the Little Ringed Plover was a very rare vagrant to
Britain, with no more than a dozen records extending back to
before 1850, and only seven this century. It was, then, a considerable surprise when on 5 June 1938 a pair was found by R.C.B.
Ledlie and E.G. Pedler, apparently settling down to breed on the

drained bed of one of the Tring Reservoirs in Hertfordshire.

The late Kenneth Allsop, bird-watcher, writer and television presenter, described the events in novel form in *Adventure Lit Their Star*, an apt title, for this first pair of Little Ringed Plovers was certainly adventurous. A main road ran along one side of their home, a public footpath along the other. Forty sheep were grazing the recently grass-sown reservoir bed, which was also a favourite resort of schoolboy cricketers and of dogs. No less than 150 ornitho-notables, as well as scores of 'lesser lights', turned up to view the birds during their stay. Yet by 14 August three young had been successfully reared.

There followed a gap of six years during which Little Ringed Plovers were of more frequent occurrence, but were not proved to breed. Then in 1944 the water level at Tring was reduced again and two pairs turned up and bred. The same year also saw a pair at a Middlesex gravel pit. With few opportunities for bird-watching during the war, Little Ringed Plovers may well have been over-looked and, while it is certain that they did not breed at Tring, the chances of their having done so at nearby gravel pits seem high. Certainly gravel pits were not the attraction to bird-watchers that they are today — the events of 1944 changed that.

Gravel pits are a by-product of concrete. They are invariably found in low-lying river valleys where accumulated gravel is easily extracted and, equally invariably, flood as soon as they are worked. The booming construction industry after the war led to an enor-mous growth in demand and pits were soon opened throughout the country. The gravel beds in Middlesex were ideally situated to supply the reconstruction of London and it is there, quite near the original site at Tring, that the Little Ringed Plover gained its first major foothold.

In 1945 four pairs were located, two in Middlesex, all at gravel pits. The following year saw four pairs in that county, two at gravel pits and two more on the gravelly bed of the King George VI Reservoir, then under construction. Birds were also present in Hertfordshire, Berkshire and Kent. The expansion continued in 1947 with six pairs in Middlesex, single pairs in Berkshire and Kent, and four pairs on the bed of the William Girling reservoir then being constructed in Essex. Thereafter the increase and spread continued year by year. By 1950 there were pairs as far north as Lincolnshire

A Little Ringed Plover approaches its well-camouflaged eggs. A colonist from 1938 onwards, the demand for gravel has been crucial in creating a new habitat for the species.

and Derbyshire, and by 1959 just under a hundred pairs were located.

This spread was closely linked to the establishment of new gravel pits, for old pits are usually too flooded and quickly become too overgrown by vegetation to suit the Plover's needs. Working pits, however, are a buzz of activity with heavy and noisy machinery in constant use. Despite this, and the inevitable accidental destruction of many nests, the Little Ringed Plover has prospered and by 1972 a total of over four hundred pairs summered. A pair has bred in Scotland, but not so far in Wales, or in the West Country. Heaviest concentrations are found in London and the Midlands and though they have bred at sewage farms, reservoirs and industrial tips, the main breeding habitat remains gravel pits. This is in sharp contrast to the situation on the Continent, where Little Ringed Plovers are most frequently noted on shingle banks along major rivers. Being rare, they have inevitably attracted the attention of egg collectors, but the birds will quickly replace a lost clutch, which is just as well in view of their chosen habitat.

The spread of the Collared Dove across Europe has been so well documented, both in the literature and in popular accounts, that no more than a sketch is required here. Until 1928 it was resident in the Balkans with a range that extended eastwards to India. Then from the area around Belgrade it started spreading in a north-westerly direction. In his masterly account of the early colonization James Fisher records that within twenty-five years it was noted at 468 places in Europe where it was previously unknown, including some Scandinavian sites 1,200 miles from Belgrade. It reached Hungary in 1932 and Czechoslovakia in 1936. By 1938 it was recorded in Austria and ten years later was well established. In 1943 it was present in Germany and reached Munich by 1948. In 1949 it was breeding in Switzerland and reached the Vosges area of France the following year. Others, meanwhile, had reached Denmark in 1948 and southern Sweden in 1949 — a spectacular leap-frogging of huge uncolonized areas to the south. It was present in Holland in 1950 and the first birds arrived in Britain at Manton in Lincolnshire in 1952, the same year that it reached Norway. At the time there was some doubt about the genuine wildness of this British bird. The first breeding took place in a garden in north Norfolk in 1955, when two pairs were present. In the following season three pairs bred in the same general area, and another was present at Gomshall in Surrey. By 1957 it was breeding in Lincolnshire, Kent and in Morayshire, the latter another huge leap forward by the species. Additionally, individuals were noted in a variety of areas including Kent, Essex and the Isles of Scilly.

By 1965, ten years after first breeding, the Collared Dove was present in almost every part of England, in large areas of Wales and Scotland and most of coastal Ireland, and had even reached the Outer Hebrides and Shetland. Throughout this period it had shown a fantastic increase of 100 percent per year. Thereafter the rate of increase slowed down, due no doubt to optimum habitat being already occupied. This is a lowland bird that is very much at home

A few sticks thrown together and the Collared Dove is in business. Its spread across Europe to Britain and beyond is one of the phenomena of twentieth-century ornithology.

in towns and villages, particularly near the coast. It avoids the hills and is thus most plentiful in the south-east and Midlands. Robert Hudson put the population at 3,000 pairs in 1964 and 15,000 to 25,000 in 1970. By 1972 there were probably over 30,000 pairs, and about this time it reached the Faeroes and Iceland.

The increase and spread of a species across a whole continent is dramatic to say the least. In part it is accounted for by the extraordinary reproductive behaviour of the Collared Dove, which has an extended breeding season and a remarkable ability to tend the young of one brood while incubating eggs of the next. It is also able to live happily alongside man and finds plantings of evergreens particularly to its liking. It feeds principally on spilt grain, and the first colonizers were regularly found feeding in association with chicken in backyards. At bird gardens and such like, it may concentrate by the hundred and it is amusing to guess at the amount of money spent by the Wildfowl Trust on unintentional feeding of these birds at places like Peakirk, where huge numbers can be found.

The steady increase will doubtless continue, with birds occupying progressively more marginal habitat. On farmland, for instance, it increased its numbers by five times in the early 1970s. Gradually, however, the population will settle down and stabilize, though it would be foolish of anyone to hazard a guess at the point when such an equilibrium might be reached. These birds have already survived several hard winters without incident and may have already passed the population of their close relative the Turtle Dove, with its 125,000 pairs.

Though less dramatic, there have been several other northward spreads of birds across Europe that have finally brought birds to Britain in recent years. Other species, yet to arrive in Britain, are still spreading northwards and it is interesting to speculate as to which birds will eventually turn up to breed with us (*see* Chapter 13). Already we have been colonized by Firecrests in 1962, Serins in 1967 and Cetti's Warblers in 1972.

Once considered a rare visitor to Britain, by the late 1950s the Firecrest was a regular migrant in spring and autumn, and a fairly regular winter visitor in small numbers. It had already spread northwards across France, and had bred in Holland for the first time in 1930. It reached Denmark in 1961, and in that summer three males were discovered singing in the New Forest. In 1962 it was proved to breed for the first time and in subsequent years a small population became established. The spread was slow, however, for it was 1968 before it summered outside the Forest in Kent and Hertfordshire, and 1970 when it was found in adjacent Dorset. Meanwhile Hampshire had a maximum of twenty-seven singing in 1969. However, the species is easily overlooked and frequently confused with the similar, but more common, Goldcrest. What is more, bird-watchers are notoriously lazy about seeking out a positive identification of every twitter they hear inland in summer — a strange contrast to their behaviour in autumn, on the coast, when every such squeak is hunted down in anticipation of a rarity.

The diminutive Firecrest has still to establish itself fully as a regular breeding bird, even though forty or more pairs may have bred in a single year in the 1970s.

That many had been overlooked became evident when Leo Batten, then of the BTO, found no less than twenty-three singing males in a single Buckinghamshire wood in 1972. Three years later, in 1975, this area had forty-three singing males; there were records north to Yorkshire and a total of between four and 121 pairs bred. This was, however, to prove a watershed in what it is hoped is the first stage of colonization.

The following year the total of singing males at the main Buckinghamshire site dropped dramatically from forty-six to eleven; there were fourteen in 1977, but only one bird, that mated with a Goldcrest and reared two hybrid young in 1978. Even eliminating records from this site, there is no doubt that 1975 was a peak year and that thereafter the species gradually declined. In 1978 it disappeared completely from the New Forest and no more than three pairs, possibly fewer, bred in the whole of Britain. So what only three years earlier had seemed to be a successful colonization had suddenly evaporated. Once again, only time will tell if the Firecrest will eventually establish itself as a regular British breeding bird.

Colonization by the Serin has been, if anything, even more hesitant. At the beginning of the last century this attractive little green and yellow finch spread northwards and eastwards from its native home in Iberia, Greece and the shores of the Mediterranean. During the following hundred years it occupied most of France, the southern half of Germany, Czechoslovakia, and much of Poland and Hungary. The fact that it did not spread from its established range in Greece into European Turkey or adjacent Bulgaria indicates that the colonization originated in Iberia and southern France rather than in the population as a whole. By 1925 it had reached the southern shores of the Baltic and was within striking distance of the Channel coast of France. By 1960 it was present in Brittany and southern Holland, but had made even greater extensions eastward into the Baltic states of the Soviet Union and southwards through Romania and Bulgaria. During the ten years prior to 1970 its spread was slower, though the number of countries in which it bred for the first time form a substantial list. It bred in Denmark, Sweden, Finland, in the environments of Leningrad and for the first time in Britain.

When the *Handbook of British Birds* was first published, in 1938, Witherby could report no more than thirty occurrences in England and two each in Scotland and Ireland. Twelve of these were from the Sussex coast, where he cautiously added 'where also small flock said to have been seen'. Bannerman had little to add but a couple of Welsh records when he wrote in 1953. After 1960 records started to increase, particularly in the southern counties, and in 1967 the species bred for the first time in Dorset. It bred again in 1969, this time in Sussex, but during the *Atlas* years of 1968–72 only five other possible breedings were discovered, including one in the Channel Isles. The early 1970s were a blank, though birds turned up from time to time at various places in southern England, totalling 235 between 1973 and 1977. Then in 1978 a pair reared two broods in

Seemingly poised for colonization, Serins bred and then withdrew across the Channel. Their eventual establishment seems certain, though the timing remains unsure.

Devonshire, with birds present at two other sites; a further pair was present in Worcestershire.

Clearly the Serin is taking its time in colonizing Britain, for unlike the Firecrest, this is an obvious bird, frequently nesting in gardens and around the outskirts of villages, and is not easily overlooked. It can be expected to turn up with increasing frequency in all southern counties and especially those bordering the Channel from Devon to Kent.

Cetti's Warbler, too, was once confined to the shores of the Mediterranean, where it inhabits tangled bushes and scrub alongside water. Like the Serin, though for different reasons, it is a difficult bird to overlook. Whereas the Serin is a brightly-coloured bird with a pleasant jingling little song, Cetti's Warbler is a dull brown, skulking bird, but with an explosive song. Its progress northwards during the early part of the present century was well documented. By 1927 it had reached the Loire and five years later it was noted near Paris. It is, however, a resident throughout its range and a series of bitter winters culminating in 1947 held its expansion in check. However, by the 1960s it was present in northern France and bred in Belgium in 1962. It appeared in Germany in the early 1960s and Holland in 1968, though breeding was not proved until 1974 and 1975 respectively. In the Channel Islands, where it had first appeared in 1960, breeding was proved in 1973.

The first British bird was present in Hampshire in the spring of 1961 and there was immediate hope of breeding. The bird disappeared, however, to be followed in 1962 by one in Sussex in October. There was then a frustrating gap of five years until a bird spent the late summer and autumn in Buckinghamshire in 1967. The following year birds were present in Sussex, Kent, Somerset and in Cork, but then once again there was a gap, this time of two years.

In 1971 Cetti's Warbler again appeared in Britain and in 1972 breeding was proved for the first time in Kent. The subsequent history of the species in this country has been extraordinary and may even rival the Collared Dove in speed of colonization. In 1973 it was present at six or seven Kentish spots and also in Norfolk and Suffolk. A total of between one and fourteen pairs bred. Numbers were similar the following year, but in 1975 between eight and seventy-five pairs were found. Numbers were maintained in 1976, but in 1977 another leap forward produced thirteen to 154 pairs spread along almost the whole of the coast of southern England and East Anglia. Additionally there was a single bird as far north as Worcestershire.

In 1978 the number of sites at which these birds were present increased from forty-one to forty-six and a total of thirty to 174 pairs bred. This included no less than 107 singing males in Kent, over seventy of which were at the main site where breeding was first proved. Though this is a well-known bird spot and a nature reserve, its name remains unpublished — presumably for fear of egg collectors or perhaps over-enthusiastic bird-watchers. One might certainly make out a case at this stage of a new species' colonization for making the whereabouts of at least one colony public, so that those who, quite naturally, will want to see the birds, can do so under controlled access. However, it may be argued that keen bird-watchers already know where to go. I have little doubt that the egg-collecting fraternity also shares that knowledge and that British-taken Cetti's Warbler eggs are already resting in the cabinets of several of these vandals. Like the other colonizers Cetti's Warbler is included in Schedule 1 of the Protection of Birds Acts, 1954–67, and thus is specially protected. Though the birds may suffer during a hard winter, and indeed did so in the winter of 1978/9, there seems little doubt that they are here to stay and that they will increase and spread.

Two other species, both gulls, have bred in Britain for the first time in recent years, though in their case the evidence of a long-term spread across Europe is more elusive. When Witherby produced the relevant volume of *The Handbook of British Birds* in 1941, he was able to list 'ten or more' records, including a small battery from the notorious Hastings area in 1915, of Mediterranean Gulls in Britain. By the 1960s this gull was established as a regular visitor in small numbers, with some individuals making an appearance year after year at favoured localities and staying on through the winter. No doubt the much-improved identification skills of the new army of bird-watchers had much to do with the increasing regularity of occurrence, for Mediterranean Gulls are easily overlooked among the vast flocks of Black-headed and other gulls that frequent our coasts. However, the increase was a real one and, as birds were soon appearing in summer as well, speculation about their possible breeding was soon abroad.

Then, in 1968, birds were seen among a huge colony of Black-headed Gulls at Needs Oar Point in Hampshire. After careful searching among thousands of nests, a pair of Mediterranean Gulls was eventually found and breeding was proved for the first time. Hybrid Mediterranean/Black-headed Gulls were also found and proved to be interbreeding with pure Black-headed Gulls on this and subsequent occasions. Indeed, these cross-bred pairs became the rule in the years that followed and it was not until 1976 that another pure pair of Mediterranean Gulls was located again. In 1977 a pure pair nested, while another seemed to be about to do so, but instead occupied the nest of a Black-headed Gull for a few days in May. It was interesting, however, that these two pairs were found in separate counties. In 1978 adults and hybrids were present but did not nest. Pure pairs appeared in three counties in 1979, including Hampshire, where eggs were laid, and Suffolk, where a pair displayed. In the third county two chicks were eventually reared. Thus 1979 saw the fourth and fifth breedings confirmed.

This, then, is the history of the Mediterranean Gull in Britain. It follows the earlier nesting of birds in Hungary and Holland and perhaps, like several other species, hybridization is virtually inevitable with a scarce colonizing bird. Meanwhile it nested in Austria, and in 1978 a colony of twenty-five pairs was discovered at Comacchio near Ravenna, constituting the first breeding in Italy.

No doubt, like other gulls, the Mediterranean has enjoyed a population boom in recent years and the spread is the inevitable result. Aware of their field characteristics, (they are not difficult to separate from other gulls at any season), bird-watchers have proved them to be regular visitors, particularly outside the breeding season. Most are discovered around our coastlines, but several have been found inland at reservoirs and rubbish tips, and one or two have even frequented a village pond in a suburban area of Surrey near London. Now it remains to be seen whether or not a pure-bred population can establish itself in Britain. They are best looked for in summer among large coastal colonies of Black-headed Gulls in southern England, but there seems no reason why they should not become established anywhere in Britain. At present they must be regarded as being in the early stages of colonization.

No doubt the Little Gull too is only in the early stages of moving into the country. However, unlike the previous species this bird has been a regular visitor, mainly in autumn, for many years, and at favoured spots occurs in good numbers. The areas of Budden Burn in Fife and Hurworth Burn in Northumberland have been noted for autumn concentrations for many years, presumably of Danish and Swedish birds passing onwards to winter.

Little Gulls pass through southern and eastern England in spring with a fair amount of regularity and there has always been some hope that eventually they might stay on and breed with us. It was not, however, until 1975 that the first eggs were laid: with eminent good sense the birds chose the well-protected and watched Ouse Washes on the Norfolk-Cambridgeshire border. Already home to a strong population of Black-tailed Godwits, a growing colony of Ruffs, and the occasional pair of Black Terns, the Ouse Washes had by 1975 become virtually a string of nature reserves. The addition of breeding Little Gulls completed the Danish-type avifauna that summer, when all four species were present and breeding. It did not require great imagination on the part of observers to envisage the Washes as the British equivalent of the marshes of Vejlerne in northern Jutland.

The spring of 1975 was an exceptionally wet one, and the Ouse Washes suffered an extraordinary degree of flooding from the middle of May well into June. Up to five Little Gulls were present and on 11 June an adult landed at the edge of a colony of Black-headed Gulls and did not re-emerge. Two days later a sub-adult was seen at the same spot and a search revealed a nest with three eggs. Some ten days later two eggs were found to be broken and an adult was found dead about a mile away. Brown rats were thought to be the culprits.

The observers concerned looked forward with anticipation to the following season, though, there being little evidence of an increase or spread elsewhere in Europe, it was thought that this might well have been a freak occurrence.

Regrettably, their hopes were dashed. Not only were there no Black Terns or Little Gulls on the Ouse Washes, but there were none elsewhere either. If the reader notes a similarity between this situation and the story of the recolonization by Avocets at Minsmere and Mediterranean Gulls at Needs Oar Point then it is perhaps no accident. Initial colonization, it seems, is an erratic business at all times.

In 1977 Little Gulls were present at an unnamed site. But though there were two adults and five immatures they did not breed. One of the adults was seen carrying nesting material and attempting to mate with an immature, so perhaps fate had brought together two adults of the same sex. For two consecutive years Little Gulls failed to breed, but the early spring of 1978 looked bright enough to change all that.

In Norfolk a pair of adults had settled down to breed by the end of May accompanied by seven immatures. Their three eggs were

Diminutive, delightful and elegant, the Little Gull eventually attempted to breed in Britain after years of tantalizing flirtation. That it failed will not, one hopes, deter it from trying again.

discovered on 16 June, but they failed to hatch. Meanwhile in Yorkshire, at the RSPB reserve at Fairburn Ings, virtually alongside the main A1 road, another pair was discovered displaying and nest building. All looked well, but early in June one of the birds was found injured, possibly by vandals, and its mate abandoned the attempted breeding and moved away. Predators destroyed the unattended nest. So both the second and third nestings of the Little Gull in Britain had failed, despite the efforts of the warden and his team of watchers. In view of the number of immatures that now summer in Britain further attempts seem likely, but the threats to rare breeding birds remain as serious as ever. One can only hope that Little Gulls will persevere with their attempts at nesting and continue patronizing the nature reserves of the RSPB and other conservation bodies.

So eight distinct species have colonized Britain for the first time from the south (interpreted in its widest sense, i.e., not north) during the present century, and there are doubtless more to come. Some like the Collared Dove and Cetti's Warbler arrived with a bang, and quickly became established. Others like the Little Ringed Plover and Black Redstart gradually built up their numbers before becoming regular. Others still seemed to be well established like the Firecrest, before virtually disappearing. While others have bird-watchers and conservationists biting their nails season after season.

Chapter Eleven

The Colonizers
—the North

A barely perceptible drop in spring and summer temperatures has been offered as the main cause of a colonization of northern Scotland by Scandinavian species while, at the same time, there has been a complementary decline in several southern species. Both factors fit nicely together and form a neatly-packaged theory. While it is easy to offer the gradual reduction of temperature as an explanation for both movements it may not be the whole story, especially in consideration of the colonization of quite different species from the south. However, even if temperature were the main factor involved, it would presumably only take a reversal of this process (that is, a gradual increase in spring and summer temperature) to send Scandinavian colonists scurrying back to their arctic forests and a whole host of southern birds northward into England. It is at the margins of their range that species are most sensitive to change and to regard the colonists from the north as anything but temporary would be the height of folly. Their colonization is of a quite different character from that of Collared Dove or Little Ringed Plover, for example.

Of all the colonists from the north the Redwing was not only the first, but also the most successful. It started to breed regularly only in the late 1950s, but by 1972 it was estimated that there were some three hundred pairs in Scotland. Thereafter the decline was as dramatic as the colonization had been. By 1978 it was present at only seven sites and there was only one case of confirmed breeding. A stark contrast with the twelve to forty-two confirmed pairs of 1972. So what had been regarded, quite justifiably, as a successful colonization subsequently fizzled out. Such are the vagaries of birds nesting at the very edge of their range.

The first nesting of Redwings in Britain was in Sutherland in 1925. There were other records in Morayshire in 1932 and 1933, and in the latter year in Sutherland, where one of the adults was killed by a hawk. All were unsuccessful. In 1935 a pair reared young on Fair Isle and it is interesting to note that these birds were believed to be of the larger and darker Icelandic sub-species *Turdus iliacus coburni*. From their first breeding in 1925 until 1966 Redwings bred in only seventeen years. Then in 1967 (what a great year that was with first records of Snowy Owl and Fieldfare) no less than seven pairs were discovered. And in 1968 there were twenty pairs in Wester Ross alone. The next landmark was 1971, when twelve pairs were proved to breed, with twenty to forty more pairs holding territory, and a further thirty males singing.

It is interesting to speculate on the origins of this colonization. Though Redwings are very difficult to separate sub-specifically in the field many of the Scottish pairs were seen by highly skilled and competent observers. Their overall opinion is that most, if not all, were of the continental race.

A Redwing at its nest in a conifer. Its colonization is part of the increasing spread of Scandinavian birds into Scotland, though its progress may have suffered a hiccup.

The number of pairs found between 1968 and 1972 was undoubtedly boosted by the *Atlas* Project, that had observers scouring even the remote Highlands in their search for breeding birds. But good totals were also found in subsequent years until 1975 when ten to thirty-four pairs bred. The following year was a disaster with only two to seven pairs and similarly low numbers have been recorded since.

Other species from the north have followed the Redwing in their colonization, but to date none have increased so dramatically and none have declined so disastrously. It is interesting to speculate that the Redwing is perhaps the most sensitive to climatic changes — first to come, first to go — but that is pure speculation.

The breeding of the Wood Sandpiper in Britain has for long been a subject of speculation. As long ago as 1846 Gurney and Fisher noted that a female and a recently-fledged juvenile had been shot near Beachamwell in Norfolk a few years earlier. Then in 1853 that noted collector John Hancock took time off from his forays in Scotland in search of Ospreys to explore Prestwick Carr in Northumberland. There, on 3 June, he found the first nest and eggs of the Wood Sandpiper in Britain. He killed the male, presumably being able to confirm the identification on dissection. The eggs were also collected. This exceptional record followed a particularly severe spring. The same observer found a Wood Sandpiper displaying at Gosforth Lake, also in Northumberland, on 10 May 1857 and presumed that it was breeding in the area. That record, however, remains in doubt.

A hundred years were to pass before another pair of Wood Sandpipers decided to settle in Britain. On this occasion they chose the much more typical wastes of Sutherland, where recently-fledged young, still with down on their heads, were discovered by Ian Downhill and G. Hallas on 23 July 1959. A pair bred in the same marsh from 1960 to 1962 and continued to do so, with occasional breaks, into the 1970s.

Opposite. *Once, and only once, a small number of Black-winged Stilts overshot their Mediterranean breeding grounds to find a suitable home on a sewage farm in England's north Midlands.*

Then in 1960 Mr and Mrs R. Cook and R. Cameron discovered a nest and four eggs in western Inverness on 10 June, and in 1961 there was a second pair in Sutherland. During the *Atlas* period there were records from many parts of the Highlands and even one in the Outer Hebrides. The maximum number of pairs was only five proved breeding in 1972, but that year there were at least fifteen adults present. The most recent data is of two to five pairs breeding in 1977 and no less than four to ten pairs in 1978, with birds present at seven sites. Clearly the colonization is getting under way and the Wood Sandpiper is now established as a regular breeding bird, though in 1979 only two pairs bred.

Of all the colonists — the Osprey was a recolonizer — none was more spectacular nor aroused so much interest as the Snowy Owl. Like so many other arctic breeding birds its population tends to rise and fall in cycles, largely dependent on the equally cyclical lemming. The well-known rush southwards, frequently to death, of the lemming is triggered off by a successful breeding season followed by high numbers and a shortage of food. When the lemmings disappear the Snowy Owls, as well as other birds such as the Rough-legged Buzzard, are left with no alternative but to follow or starve. Thus there were huge irruptions in North America in 1917–18, 1926–7, 1934–5, 1941–2 and 1945–6. In the 1926–7 irruption several thousand birds were recorded in the United States and many hitched lifts on ships to reach Britain.

During the nineteenth century the Snowy Owl was a comparatively regular winter visitor to Britain, especially to Shetland. It was first recognized by Dr Lawrence Edmundston in 1808 in Orkney, and first collected by him in the spring of 1812. The specimen was sent to Mr Bullock in London, who noted that the female had been shot a few weeks earlier. Bullock was sure that

---

1
2

1 A male Red-backed Shrike at its increasingly rare nest in southern England. Yet, as its numbers decline in the south, so there is an encouraging increase in Scotland.
2 Escapees from bird collections have managed to survive nearby in the wild, thus establishing Reeve's Pheasant as a potentially new British bird. Even a series of hard winters have not eliminated this species.

Snowy Owls bred in Shetland, but Dr Edmundston was decidedly sceptical. There had been reports of adults with well-fledged young, but none were authenticated.

Gradually the Snowy Owl became a rarer and rarer visitor and by the early part of the twentieth century it was virtually a vagrant. Then from 1963 onwards the occasional bird started to reappear in Shetland, as well as elsewhere in Scotland. Mostly these were the almost pure white male birds, but early in 1967 Bobby Tulloch, RSPB Shetland Representative, saw a female as well. Then on 7 June 1967, while showing eleven Swiss bird-watchers over the island, he 'found a Snowy Owl's nest with three eggs on Stakkaberg' as he blandly recorded in his diary. Now Bobby has always struck me as a remarkably cool man, but this bald statement can hardly have done justice to his feelings as he crouched over the first-ever British nest of the Snowy Owl.

The nest was placed on an open hill on the island of Fetlar, the 'green island' of Shetland. Bobby's first inclinations were to keep it secret at least until the young had flown, but Fetlar has a crofting population and is justly popular among bird-watchers for other scarce birds that breed there. The chances of accidental disturbance and too many bird-watchers was real enough, but there were the egg collectors to consider as well. If these extraordinary vandals and thieves were prepared to have a go at the well-guarded Ospreys then think of the kudos of a clutch of British-taken Snowy Owl eggs.

In collaboration with the RSPB and with the help of local friends, Bobby managed to get an observation post erected and a round-the-clock watch established. Volunteers and an RSPB staff member kept a careful vigil, noting every coming and going and the Secretary of State for Scotland, in conjunction with the landowner, granted a Sanctuary Order. Eventually the eggs hatched: the news was made public and was well covered by the media. The birds were photographed by Eric Hosking at the invitation of the RSPB and a film was shot by local photographer Dennis Coutts, whose main occupation was local weddings and 'occasions'. Ultimately five youngsters flew from the clutch of seven eggs, a high success rate by any standards.

Whether 1967 had been a freak year or not was hotly debated but, in the hope of a repeat performance the following year, Tulloch and the RSPB began making a more elaborate set of arrangements so

One of the most extraordinary events of modern British ornithology was the discovery of a pair of Snowy Owls nesting on the island of Fetlar in Shetland.

that the 'guardians' of Britain's most exclusive family could enjoy a little more comfort, and the anticipated hordes of Snowy Owl-watchers could get better views with as little disturbance to the birds as possible. Once again, a pair, presumably the same birds, nested in 1968. Nesting followed in each of the next seven years, and though they never managed five again a grand total of twenty-one young Snowy Owls flew. In 1973 two females established nests and there were high hopes of an expanding population. But the lone male was unable to hunt successfully enough to provide for two females and the new and younger female deserted her three eggs. The following year she tried once more, but this time gave up after laying only one egg. In 1975 Snowy Owls bred again, but for the last time. The male, presumably the original bird of 1967, disappeared and was not replaced. Since then females have regularly been present on Fetlar and elsewhere in Shetland, but the lack of a male has prevented breeding. In 1977, for instance, at least five females were present on Fetlar, and two at another site. But in 1978 and 1979 only two females were present on Fetlar, though a male popped in to nearby Fair Isle in April.

It has been suggested that the males, being considerably smaller than their mates, are more susceptible to cold and find hunting the rabbits, on which they depend, more difficult. Certainly many more female chicks have survived than males. As a result, the idea of importing one or more males has gained considerable support. But the artificiality of such an introduction seems a deliberate inter-ference with nature. If Snowy Owls are to be introduced then a case can be made for introducing a whole range of other species to augment the British avifauna. While reintroductions of birds that man has eliminated seem acceptable, the introduction of new species destroys the natural processes which ornithologists find so fascinating. Eventually Britain could become a gigantic zoo full of exotics to the ultimate detriment of our native fauna. One day, perhaps, a male will struggle across the North Sea and meet up with the presumably eager females of Shetland. Then once again the Snowy Owl will breed in Britain. The fact that they did so success-fully from 1967 to 1975 is a tribute to the RSPB and to Bobby Tulloch.

The year 1967 was also notable for the first ever breeding of Field-fares. That year birds were present throughout the country in good winter numbers and many stayed on very late. The result was a nest found in June in Orkney from which three young birds flew, and the possibility of nesting in Durham where two adults and three juveniles were seen in July. The next year, and the following two years saw the first breeding in Shetland, when two or three pairs nested among those islands. In 1970 a nest in eastern Inverness was the first for the Scottish mainland, and in 1969 and 1970 there were nests as far south as Derbyshire. By 1974, though numbers remained small, there were records from various parts of the High-lands and the Pennines. By the time the *Atlas* was prepared the editors were able to show a scattering of breeding records from Shetland to Staffordshire, and in 1976 between three and nine pairs nested.

A pair of Fieldfares at their nest in a birch. While Scandinavian birds bred in Scotland, their continental counterparts moved into northern England – a two-pronged colonization.

That this was not a simple case of colonization from Scandinavia became evident when birds appeared in Kent and Suffolk. For over a century the Fieldfare has been gradually extending its range westwards across Europe. It spread into what is now West Germany towards the end of last century and reached Switzerland in 1923. Thirty years later it nested in the Jura of eastern France, and in 1965 in Denmark for the first time. In 1967 it reached Belgium, the same year that it was found nesting in Orkney. A glance at the *Atlas* map is sufficient to indicate (though not to prove) that two populations may be involved; one from Scandinavia colonizing Scotland north of Perth, the other from England south of the border. If 1978 saw a halt to this 'two-pronged' colonization, this may well be only a hiccup in a gradual westwards spread.

*   *   *

Though decidedly more scarce on passage than the Little Stint, Temminck's Stint breeds much further to the south, and at no great distance from northern Scotland on the Norwegian Dovrefjell. It is, then, not surprising that it is the scarcer Temminck's Stint that has, on occasion, stopped to breed with us, rather than the sometimes abundant, and certainly regular, Little Stint.

In recent years Temminck's Stints, like Wood Sandpipers, have colonized Scotland and seem to be getting established. Their numbers remain small, but they are regular at least in one area. This colonization can be regarded as a southwards (or westwards) extension of range by a Scandinavian species, due perhaps to the changing climate of northern Europe in recent decades. But Temminck's Stint nested sporadically in Britain long before this period of change began.

The first nest was discovered near a small Cairngorms' lochan, on 13 June 1934, by George Edwards, who was walking and birding the hills with Vernon Crapnell. Both saw the adults, but the four eggs were well bedded into the base of the nest, and following heavy rain over the next couple of days, they were damp, cold and apparently deserted. The eggs were then taken and subsequently shown by Dr P.R. Lowe at a meeting of the British Ornithologists' Club in October 1934. Birds were present in 1935, though no nest was found.

The following year again saw George Edwards on Cairngorms, where he had the good fortune to discover the second Temminck's Stint nest. The following day Edwards found that one of the eggs had disappeared: it was discovered with a hole in it some distance from the nest. The adult was, however, incubating and Edwards and Crapnell erected a hide to film the sitting bird. Unfortunately the Stint then deserted the nest, a fact that brought a stern rebuke from the editors of *British Birds*. Evidently Ralph Chislett had previously warned the discoverers not to attempt filming before the eggs had hatched but, as the editors of *British Birds* were well aware, young waders leave the nest soon after hatching and would then have been impossible to film. Whether or not the desertion was caused by filming remains unknown and unknowable, but Edwards thought the eggs were infertile anyway. It is easy to argue, after the event, that a rare nesting bird should be left alone to get on with the business of rearing its brood, but waders are notoriously tame and

A couple of small colonies of this tiny Scandinavian sandpiper are established in northern Scotland and the Temminck's Stint can now be properly regarded as a British bird.

approachable on their breeding grounds and have suffered far greater indignity than filming over the years without apparent harm.

The next nesting took place well to the south, among the Yorkshire Moors. On 1 July 1951 A. Lee and S. Jackson noticed a Temminck's Stint performing a distraction display feigning a broken wing. Careful searching revealed a neat nest containing four eggs. On 3 July it was seen by Ralph Chislett, who coincidentally had been one of the major critics of Edwards and Crapnell fifteen years earlier. The adult was found dead on 12 July, having been killed by a rat or weasel, and the well-set eggs were removed to the York Museum.

Five years later, in 1956, Temminck's Stints returned to Scotland, where they were discovered in the Spey Valley by Desmond

Nethersole-Thompson. On 19 May, near a loch over 1,000 feet above sea level, he discovered a Stint calling from the top of a conifer. The bird performed a song flight, and then, on 29 May, a Stint was noted creating a scrape, while its mate stood nearby. On 16 June a nest with four eggs was found, but they had disappeared by the following day without trace. Perhaps they had been collected, though this remains unproved.

After thirteen years of absence, Temminck's Stints returned once more to Scotland in 1969. On this occasion, and in subsequent years, disturbance was kept to an absolute minimum. One or two pairs were present at one site in Easter Ross between 1969 and 1971, but it was not until 16 July 1971, when two down-covered chicks were seen, that breeding was actually proved. The birds returned in subsequent years, and by 1977 four or five were noted displaying. In 1978 breeding was proved in two counties, with up to ten individuals involved. Eggs were deserted at one site, but at the main site the outcome remains unknown. Though probably successful, it was decided that even the disturbance caused by attempting to prove the record was too dangerous, a welcome turn-about from the old collecting days.

Goldeneye breed among the lakes and forests of the conifer zone from Scandinavia across Siberia and North America. They invariably choose a hole at some height in a tree for their nest and the ducklings have to jump to the ground soon after hatching and follow their mother up to two or three miles to the water she has selected as home. Thus it came as a shock when, instead of nesting in a tree in Scotland, the first Goldeneye to breed in Britain occupied a rabbit burrow near Burton on the Dee estuary in Cheshire in 1931. The nest and eggs of this first record were collected, and the event written up by F. Taylor in the Bulletin of the British Oologists' Association in 1938. Such was the reception meted out to any bird that attempted to depart from the norm. However, in 1932 the Goldeneye pair attempted to breed again in the same location, and again in a rabbit burrow. Such a freak occurrence must have been the result of unusual circumstances and it seems likely that one, or both, of the birds was pricked (wounded by shot) and unable to migrate northwards.

Following this extraordinary occurrence there was no further breeding until 1970. Meanwhile birds continued to summer in Ireland and especially Scotland. Courtship was regularly noted even as late as June, but the birds were regarded as non-breeders, or conceivably late migrants. The difficulties of finding a Goldeneye nest can be imagined and proof of breeding inevitably depends on finding a female with young. And so it was in 1970 when a duck with four ducklings was discovered on a small loch in Inverness. In 1971 a nest with empty shells and two infertile eggs was discovered, and in the following year a duck with nine youngsters was seen on 28 May. In 1973 three pairs bred and a similar number the following year.

There can be no doubt that the colonization of Scotland by the Goldeneye is yet another example of an extension of range by a Scandinavian species. Yet though so much of Scotland, with its lochs and conifer forests, would seem to offer ideal habitat, there is a great scarcity of suitable natural, or large woodpecker holes. Fortunately Goldeneye take readily to nest boxes and the erection of these in suitable sites has undoubtedly been a significant factor in the colonization. Certainly in the years 1973 and 1974 five out of six nests were in special Goldeneye boxes. By 1977 there were six or seven nests and in 1978 no less than thirteen in the Highland region. However, 1979 proved to be an absolute Goldeneye bonanza, with twenty-two to forty pairs rearing at least 110 youngsters, more than double the previous best total.

The history of the 1978 nests is of considerable interest: of the thirteen only two were in natural sites, the rest in nest boxes. But of the eleven in boxes, two were robbed by egg collectors. So the Goldeneye and its protectors face, to use a recent cliché, 'Catch 22'. As natural holes are scarce the species requires nest boxes to aid colonization, but nest boxes are obvious to collectors and a significant proportion will be robbed. Perhaps it will be possible to construct a collector-proof box in the way that the Post Office has designed a vandal-proof telephone box. We have woodpecker-proof nest boxes made of concrete and rubber; perhaps an indestructible disposable box might be the answer. In any case the Goldeneye seems well established in Scotland and, provided boxes are erected elsewhere, there is no reason why it should not spread over large areas of the Highlands.

*   *   *

The first recorded summering of Shore Larks was noted by P.J. Coe and P.A.M. Gepp while bird-watching in Scotland on 6 July 1972. The bird was watched singing from the ground; indeed, but for its song it may well have been overlooked, as it merged well with its broken surroundings. Lacking 'horns' — in America the bird is more appropriately called Horned Lark — it was thought to be a male in its first summer. The following year both Coe and Gepp visited the area again, but neither could find the bird. Then on 24 June a bird was discovered less than a mile away by an anonymous observer, while on the 10 July A. Watson and T.P. Milsom located a pair just over half a mile from the other two sites. Careful searching revealed nothing more.

On 14 August Watson discovered yet another pair at a different site just over a mile away. Once again it was the voice that aided discovery, though on this occasion only a single sharp call of alarm was given — both birds were within four yards, far too close for binoculars. Watson, startled as he was, noticed a 'much smaller, scurrying dark brown object which I assumed to be a chick and which stayed so close that it seemed to be at the adult's heels'. The 'object' was in view for less than two seconds, but as he stood and watched the adults, fearful of moving for fear of treading on the chick, he heard cheeping calls from two different directions. Carefully, and after only six minutes of observation, Watson withdrew.

Mr Watson returned the following day with Dr Adam Watson and both observers watched the adults and listened to cheeping from the presumed chicks. Once more, however, they failed to find them — and alert to the dangers of tramping in search of them they withdrew. Then on 18 August Mr Watson returned again, this time in company with N. Picozzi. Once again the chicks were heard and the female was seen carrying food. On 21 August the Watsons, Mr and Dr, together with Roy Dennis, returned to the area but could find no trace of the birds. In his paper on the events Mr Watson uses the title 'Shore Larks summering and possibly breeding in Scotland'. On the evidence of that paper alone I regard breeding as proved beyond, as they say, any reasonable doubt; the first occasion for Britain.

In 1974 and 1975 there were no reports of the birds, but in 1976 they summered again. Then in 1977 Shore Larks were present in two areas of Scotland. One held a single adult on 23 June. At the other, two or three males were found singing in June and the first British nest, containing three eggs, was discovered on 25 June. Later, in August and early September, at least one juvenile was present.

Inevitably there is a certain amount of secrecy about the nesting of such rare birds, and locations and even names of observers are frequently withheld from publication. Mr Watson's initial discovery had, however, been followed by other visiting observers and soon the grapevine was in action. In the circumstances it was thought better that the event should be made public rather than hidden among clouds of uncertainty. There were no reports in 1978 or 1979.

When Ian Cumming took his family for a walk up a Scottish mountain on 19 June 1977, he little thought that he was to add yet another species to the list of British breeding birds. Ostensibly they were on the look-out for Ptarmigan, but while walking at over 3,000 feet among rough grass and heather Ian spotted a male Lapland Bunting. A few minutes later he noticed that there was also a female, so well camouflaged that he had previously overlooked her. The female begged, unsuccessfully, for food from her mate and Ian realized that breeding was a possibility. As the Cumming family walked away they flushed a small bird from the grass, and it was Mrs Cumming who found the first nest of Lapland Bunting in Britain.

Unfortunately the nest was empty, but Ian returned to the mountain on 26 June, to find that it held a clutch of four eggs. He searched the rest of the area and found a second nest fifty yards away, similarly holding four eggs. So Lapland Buntings had actually bred. Ten days later he returned once more, this time in company with Roy Dennis, the RSPB representative. Both nests were once again located and found to contain young about five days old. Returning finally on 17 July Ian found both nests empty, but failed to locate the birds in thick cloud and heavy rain.

During his visits Ian photographed both nests, the lone male that seemed to be mated with both females, and the male together with

A female Lapland Bunting at its nest. The colonization of a few Scottish hills was something of a surprise to British ornithologists as they speculated about future colonists from Scandinavia.

one of the females. Despite being a popular walking hill, with Black-headed Gulls nearby, the Lapland Buntings were well camouflaged and easily overlooked. There seems no reason to doubt that the young were successfully reared.

The winter of 1976–7 had been severe with snow remaining on the ground exceptionally late. Even in June, when the Lapland Buntings were first discovered, snow was plentiful and still melting. Only once before, in 1974, when a male was discovered in Caithness on 30 June, had a Lapland Bunting been observed in summer in suitable breeding habitat.

The year 1977 had also seen Lapland Buntings in other parts of Scotland. Indeed, when all the records from different observers were collected together it was realized that no less than six different sites had been occupied, at one of which no less than six males and a single female had been observed. All told, no less than twenty-three Lapland Buntings had summered, though the only nests discovered were those found by the Cumming family.

Though Ian Cumming was unsuccessful in finding his Lapland Buntings in 1978, three sites were occupied elsewhere. At one, three pairs were present and a nest (the third in British history) was discovered on 28 June. Later young birds were seen in the area. Elsewhere a pair built a nest, but eggs were not laid. So Lapland Buntings had returned to Scotland after a much warmer spring than 1977. In 1979 birds were present at two sites, and though breeding was not proved, three pairs may have bred. It remains to be seen whether this is the beginning of a colonization, or another of those freak occurrences that grace British ornithology from time to time.

By 1978 ornithologists were becoming quite used to the idea that new breeding birds were colonizing Scotland from Scandinavia and considerable speculation was generated over a few jars at 'locals' up and down the country about which species would be next to arrive. Some favoured Turnstone, others Sanderling, others still Jack Snipe. In the event, 1978 brought the Purple Sandpiper, a name not on many lips the previous winter.

A pair was first discovered 'somewhere in Scotland' on 3 June. They were still present on 20 June and were seen again on 26 June. Then on 8 July an adult was noted performing the strange 'rodent run' (the Purple Sandpiper equivalent of the 'broken-wing' distraction display of the plovers), and three down-covered chicks were discovered. On 29 July an adult was present with a flying juvenile. So far only this sparse information has been disclosed; there was no evidence of breeding in 1979.

The first known nesting of Bramblings in Britain occurred in 1920 as reported by C. and T.E. Hodgkin. The observers were remarkably fortunate, for they were able to note that nest building commenced on 19 May, and that seven eggs had been laid by the end of that month. They were taken on 7 June. Thereafter there are no fully-documented records until 1979, though birds were said to have bred meanwhile in Inverness, Perth and Ross among other places. As recently as 1976 the *Atlas* could add nothing to the story save only that a hybrid Brambling x Chaffinch chick had been found, that a female had been trapped for ringing with a pronounced brood-patch, and that there were four instances of males singing in summer. Of this motley collection of 'possibilities', three were in Scotland, one in northern England and two in south-central England.

On 23 June 1979 in the new Grampian Region (even more vague than the old county system) Stephen Buckland found a female Brambling feeding among birches. Suspecting breeding he returned a week later. Though he failed to find the bird he did hear a song that was unfamiliar to him and which, on checking with recordings, turned out to be that of a Brambling.

Accompanied by Alan Knox, Stephen set off on 2 July and on entering the wood immediately saw a female Brambling. It obligingly settled on its nest. As it left only briefly to feed every so often, the two observers presumed that it must be incubating. However, the nest was some twenty-five feet up and about four and a half feet from the top of a slender tree, so its contents could not be examined. Though the female was followed a couple of times by a male Chaffinch, there was also a male Brambling present in the wood so a hybrid pair seems unlikely.

On 8 July there was no activity at the nest and it was presumed deserted. Using a mirror attached to a pole the nest was inspected and at least three eggs could be seen. Finally, on 13 July Stephen Buckland found that the nest had been overturned and discovered two eggs on the ground below. One was smashed, but one was still intact and was found to contain a dead embryo. It is interesting and significant to note that, being protected by special penalties under Schedule 1 of the Protection of Birds Act 1954–67, even the fallen egg could only be removed under licence. There were also birds of both sexes present in Shetland, indicating a total of four possible breeding pairs. The spring of 1979 was certainly one of the coldest this century and the discoverers of the 1979 nest believe that this, plus the exceptional number of Bramblings the previous winter, accounts for their record. It does, however, seem equally likely that this is yet another example of the colonization of Scotland by a Scandinavian species. Once again, time will tell.

In 1973 and 1974 pairs of Sanderlings were present in summer on Scottish mountain tops, though there was no proof of breeding. Sanderlings do not breed as far south as Scandinavia, let alone

Scotland. Turnstones act increasingly suspiciously at suitable breeding sites in the far north, though as yet they have never been proved to breed. A Glaucous Gull has paired with a Herring Gull every year since 1975 in Shetland, producing hybrid young. Perhaps one year it will be fortunate enough to discover another adult Glaucous Gull and provide the first pure breeding of that species for Britain. Long-tailed Skuas have occasionally spent the summer among colonies of Arctic Skuas, but so far there is no hint of breeding. Scarlet Rosefinch and Thrush Nightingales are both increasing in Norway and may, in the future, colonize Britain. Certainly the 1980s and 1990s should prove an exciting time for summer birdwatchers in both southern England and northern Scotland.

Chapter Twelve

Once in a Lifetime

Of all the birds that have bred in Britain and Ireland, and there are over 200 regulars, there are a handful that can only be described as of freak occurrence. They are neither the early pioneers of a newly colonizing, or soon to colonize, species, nor are they the last remnants of a disappearing bird. In some cases their appearance can be explained by unusual weather circumstances, in others by little understood population dynamics; but in most cases a freak occurrence is no more than that — a once in a lifetime chance taken.

Unfortunately the history of these freak breedings goes back little further than the beginning of the present century. Though the scarce or rare bird was sought as assiduously by our grandfathers as by present-day watchers, an unusual bird was shot on sight, not watched, observed and conceivably tracked back to its nest. 'Hit' may well have been 'history', but in some cases the fact of collection may well have covered up an attempted breeding by one of our 'freaks'. So effectively we are concerned with the history of ornithology during the present century and birds that have bred erratically during that period.

Great Northern Divers have summered in Shetland and the Outer Isles for as long as man has been documenting the history of British birds. Most such birds are clearly immatures, but adults are regularly present, and breeding has been widely suspected, if not actually proved, for generations. In 1932 G. Johnson, in 1933 G.T. Kay, and in 1946 Mr and Mrs Venables all observed adults in association with young in Shetland waters — though in each case the possibility (not 'probability') of the family having swum in together could not be ruled out.

Such speculative observations continued to be made until, in late June 1970, a pair of Great Northerns with two youngsters were found on a loch in Wester Ross by E.N. Hunter. Thus breeding was proved for the first time. The following year a hybrid Great

After years of rumour and unproven reports a pair of Great Northern Divers finally bred in Scotland. Whether it was a 'one-off' only time will tell.

Northern x Black-throated paired with a pure Black-throated to produce a single chick at the same location. So the breeding of the Great Northern Diver remains erratic in Britain. Yet despite the attention it has attracted, and the remoteness of the areas that these birds inhabit, the persistency of rumoured nesting is such that the Great Northern Diver must be regarded as at least a dubious member of this strange club.

The membership of the White Stork must also be questioned, not because it is suspect of being too regular, like the Great Northern Diver, but rather because it is so erratic as to be virtually unproven. In 1416 a pair of these widespread European birds settled on the church of St Giles in Edinburgh and stayed through the season. Bannerman regards comment on a five-hundred-year-old occurrence as 'superfluous', but White Storks have spent time off-passage in Britain and, being long distance migrants, are prone to this sort of vagrancy. Inevitably there is an element of doubt that is sufficient for the scientist to dismiss the record as 'unproven'.

So I move on to the Whooper Swan, which not only has more in common with the Great Northern Diver, but also breeds with such regularity as to merit little more than a mention in this chapter. The birds certainly bred in Orkney, albeit irregularly, until the eighteenth century. During the present century there were only a handful of proven cases prior to the 1960s, since when breeding has been suspected or proved virtually every year.

Baillon's Crake is a decidedly scarce and elusive little bird that was proved to breed in Cambridge in 1858, and in Norfolk in 1866 and 1889. It may, of course, have bred in East Anglia at other times and even, perhaps, have been a regular member of the Fenland avifauna. But that is speculation. It is difficult enough to find and identify this bird, let alone prove breeding by finding the nest. Suffice it that there was not a hint of breeding during the years of the BTO's *Atlas* Project, despite an unprecedented scouring of the countryside by bird-watchers; and only two individuals had even been found as vagrants in the previous twenty years. Here, then, is either a genuine erratic, or a bird that covers its traces far too well. It seems reasonable, in view of the above, to opt for Baillon's Crake as being truly an erratic visitor to our shores that breeds once, or maybe thrice, in a lifetime.

Though the Green Sandpiper has a similar distribution to the Wood Sandpiper, if a more southerly one, it has shown no indication of joining that species in colonizing Britain. Though it regularly winters along the streams of southern England and has been noted displaying and singing in Scotland with a fair amount of regularity, nevertheless it has been proved to breed on only two occasions. The first took place in Westmorland in 1917 and rests on the observations of a gamekeeper named Waterhouse. On 10 August he discovered a pair of Green Sandpipers with two, almost feathered young. Two members of the BOU were shown the birds and one of them, H.W. Robinson, wrote an account for *British Birds*. Not surprisingly, in view of the prevalent attitude towards sight records, Mr Robinson was criticized for not having collected a specimen to prove the breeding. But he riposted well. 'Surely' he wrote in reply 'when the young, quite unable to fly, are seen with their parents, it is proof enough of their having been hatched there, without having to slaughter one or all of them to prove it.' However, some doubt about the record remained and the editor of *Ibis* similarly expressed his reservations. It was not until twenty years later that M. Garnett interviewed the Reverend E.U. Savage, who had been present with Robinson and had seen the 1917 birds. Savage makes it quite clear that not only were the adults and chicks seen, but that they were seen together as a family party. On the basis of this additional evidence the record is generally accepted.

Strangely enough there is also an element of doubt about the second record of these birds breeding in Britain. Frank Clafton, sometime warden of Portland Bird Observatory, was exploring a boggy wilderness area of Inverness in May 1959. On 29 May he and his wife identified an adult Green Sandpiper. The following day, 30 May, they found a chick, and took photographs and a full field description of it. Though adult and chick were never seen together, there seemed to be a relationship in the area occupied between them. The photographs were found to agree with Green Sandpiper chicks more than any other wader species by independent experts — so the record stands. An element of doubt, however unreasonable it may be, remains. The first 100-percent proof of breeding by this bird in Britain remains for some fortunate future observer.

The increase in the number of records of what were formerly described as 'transatlantic' vagrants has been a feature of recent years. Some species have, as a result, become accepted as regular migrants, notably Pectoral Sandpiper, but other American waders seem to be fast heading from vagrancy toward regularity. Each year sees more and more better trained eyes searching for transatlantic waifs, and new birds are being added to the British list with extraordinary rapidity. It seems likely that it is the increase in observers and their greater field expertise, rather than any change of habits by the birds, that is responsible.

For years the possible colonization by American birds has been a subject of hot debate and endless speculation. Comparatively little has been written, but over the 'odd pint' bird-watchers have argued the case of this or that species well into the night. The reasons for such debate are not obscure. Taking all records of

American waders prior to 1957, a grand total of 340 or so individuals is reached, compared with a total of 1,015 during the following fifteen years. The cautious note of the Sharrocks, that the increase merely matched that of other rarities, did little to stem speculation. Hot favourite, with nearly half the recent records to its credit, was the Pectoral Sandpiper, a species that occurs with some frequency on the east coast in early autumn, whereas most other American birds make a more 'natural' landfall in the west. Indeed, records of Pectoral Sandpipers in Africa would seem to indicate that a breeding, or at least summering, population already exists somewhere in the north-western Palearctic.

It came, therefore, as something of a shock when Gordon Wilson, a Berkshire ornithologist, announced that he had found the first ever nest of an American wader in Europe — a Spotted Sandpiper in the Highland Region of Scotland.

Mr Wilson was on holiday on the Scottish coast when, on 15 June 1975, he noticed a bird that he initially (and quite naturally) took to be a Common Sandpiper alight on a boulder at the mouth of a freshwater stream. A glance through binoculars was sufficient to reveal a heavily-spotted breast and the presence of an American Spotted Sandpiper — only the twenty-seventh for Britain and Ireland. After watching the bird for some time Mr Wilson went on his way. He returned two days later when, to his delight, the bird was still present.

Ten days later, on 27 June, he found the bird yet again. On this occasion, however, it flew off up the beach and disappeared among vegetation. Walking carefully forward Gordon Wilson flushed the bird, which flew only a few yards away before calling excitedly from a log. A quick search revealed the nest, and an equally quick withdrawal prompted the bird to return to the nest within three minutes — the record was proved.

Mr Wilson returned later with a local ornithologist and together they saw two Spotted Sandpipers. The following day another local confirmed the record. Within a day or two Mr Wilson returned southward and, informing the *British Birds'* Rare Breeding Birds Panel, Roy Dennis went along to check it out.

On 7 July one of the local observers found the nest deserted and no sign of the adults. Cattle were grazing nearby and heavy rain had fallen; one or other presumably caused the birds to desert. On 30

July Roy Dennis once again visited the nest and removed the eggs. Two were infertile, but two contained developing embryos. To date the birds have not returned and this remains the only record of a North American wader breeding in Europe.

Black-winged Stilts are large black and white birds with amazingly long pink legs — they are thus unmistakable and not easily over-looked. The fact that they have bred in Britain only on a single occasion can, therefore, be taken as completely accurate, for it is unlikely that they could nest without being discovered. These are attractive summer visitors to southern Europe that, as is the way with such species, occasionally overshoot in spring. Sometimes such invasions can lead to breeding well to the north of the normal range. In 1935, for instance, a considerable invasion in spring led to the establishment of several breeding pairs in Holland. A similar event in 1949 brought no less than ten pairs to the same country after an absence of three years. Meanwhile in 1945 a few pairs were noted in Holland and the species bred in Britain for the first and only time.

Two clutches of eggs were laid on sewage lagoons at the Notting-ham Sewage Farm in 1945. The events were described by J. Stanton and it is to the credit of the observers who watched the birds that three young Stilts eventually flew despite being flooded. A second clutch of eggs was collected by a boy before they had been discovered by the watchers. In view of their periodic invasions of Holland it seems quite likely that Stilts will some day return to breed once more in Britain — it is unlikely, however, that their appearances will ever be more than erratic.

Not so very long ago the Gull-billed Tern was virtually unknown in Britain, Holland, and in other parts of northern Europe. Whether the birds were absent or overlooked it is impossible to say, but certainly between the wars this species was more frequently noted and breeding was first proved in Holland in 1931. It was not until 1944 that the second Dutch nest was found, but thereafter there were several pairs each year. It was doubtless from this source that the birds spread to Britain in 1949.

On 24 July of that year G.A. Pyman and R.V.A. Marshall were watching birds that had established a colony on a drying-out island

When a Black-winged Stilt first visited Britain it was a notable event – when it actually bred it was amazing. Yet even so rare a bird had one of its nests vandalized by youths.

at the recently flooded Abberton Reservoir in Essex. Apart from gulls there were Common and Little Terns; Tufted, Mallard and Shoveler, Redshank, Ringed Plover and even some Great Crested Grebes that had been stranded high and dry as the water level dropped. On this particular day, however, the observers were mobbed by a pair of large terns that they subsequently identified as Gull-billed. They had come, with the Common Terns, from the direction of the island, but as they were initially thought to be Sandwich Terns the noisy pair were not followed up.

On 2 July 1950, almost a year later, Pyman again met up with these terns and within a week had decided against Sandwich and in favour of Gull-billed — a verdict to which Marshall had come quite independently. On 4 July Colonel C.B. Wainwright, who for years ran a bird observatory and ringing station at Abberton, had ringed a dark-billed tern chick while an adult Gull-billed screamed overhead. The chick was seen on several subsequent days, but was found dead on 13 July, when its identity was 'fairly obvious'. Identification was confirmed by R. Wagstaffe of the celebrated Liverpool Museum, resting place of so many rare deceased British birds. In subsequent years the island remained submerged, save for occasional late autumn appearances, and the Gull-billed Terns did not return.

Pallas's Sandgrouse breeds in the steppe region of the southern Soviet Union from the Caspian Sea eastwards. It first came to the notice of British ornithologists during a minor invasion late in 1859. The first was a male shot at Walpole St Peters near the Wash in early July. It was followed by another male shot from a flock of three at Tremadoc on Cardigan Bay on 9 July, and another obtained apparently at New Romney in Kent in November.

A far more substantial invasion occurred in 1863. The first birds were obtained from a flock of fourteen in Northumberland on 21 May, but within a few days there were flocks in many east coast counties and birds gradually spread westwards through the country. One reached the Outer Isles and was killed on 13 October on Benbecula, and several found their way to Ireland. This same invasion brought birds to many and various parts of western Europe and several nests were noted in Holland and Denmark.

Though a couple of flocks were observed in 1872 and again in 1876, it was not until 1888 that the next big irruption took place. By February huge flocks were on the move in eastern Europe and by May they had reached Britain. Thousands of birds were involved and a special Act was rushed trough Parliament to protect them. By the time it became effective in February 1889 the Pallas's Sand-grouse had been virtually wiped out by collectors. Yet some managed to breed only to have their eggs taken by the likes of Mr Swailes of Beverley in Yorkshire. Alexander Scott, a gamekeeper at Culbin Sands, found a nestling in June and the following year he obtained another which was sent to Alfred Newton who, from that specimen, published the first description of a Pallas's Sandgrouse chick. Some survived into 1889 and a few even managed to get through another winter into 1890. Indeed there were rumours of birds still present at late as 1892, but these remain undocumented.

Thereafter minor Pallas's Sandgrouse irruptions occurred in 1890, 1891 (though these may refer to the lingerers of 1888), 1899, 1904, 1906 and 1908, when another substantial movement took place. Finally there were birds in 1909, and then none until a single bird was seen at Stodmarsh in Kent, in December 1964. The causes of this sudden decline have not been fully investigated, but the ploughing up of the Russian steppes must have had a very serious effect on the birds' habitat. Certainly the breeding of these birds was a freak occurrence that, at the present time at least, seems unlikely ever to be repeated.

Every year three brightly-coloured birds of the Mediterranean overshoot on their way northward in spring to reach our shores. The Hoopoe and Golden Oriole do so with regularity and stay on to breed most years in small numbers. Somewhat less frequently the Bee-eater arrives in late May only to vanish, presumably returning whence it came. It is interesting to note that even these visitations have become more rare in recent years. However, in 1920 a pair settled down at Musselburgh just outside Edinburgh and selected a hole in a sandbank. On 11 June the female was found injured. She was cared for and laid an egg the following day, but died on 15 June and the male disappeared.

After the Musselburgh fiasco there were no further attempts to nest in northern Europe until a pair settled on the island of Born-holm in Denmark in 1948. Then on 12 June 1955 three Bee-eaters were seen in Sussex by E.A. Packington. They were naturally thought to be vagrants until, on 31 July, Miss M. Songhurst and Mr and Mrs D.E. Kimmins discovered five birds inhabiting a Sussex sand pit a couple of miles away. On 3 August Miss Songhurst, together with Mrs G. Witherington, revisited the pit and found the first ever British Bee-eater's nest. A couple of days later a second nest was discovered by Commander Charles Jack and J. Walpole-Bond and a third, partially destroyed, nesting hole was found about the same time by P. Robertson.

Clearly the news was already spreading fast via the ornitho-grapevine and, without any publication mentioning the locality, over 1,000 visitors turned up during the following four weeks. By 8 August the RSPB had been called in and the pit was watched over more or less continuously until the birds departed on 20 September. During this period the Bee-eaters were guarded by some of the top-brass of Sussex ornithology including Lord Hurcomb, G. des Forges, Kate Barham, Derek Goodwin and Bert Axell, who took time off from nearby Dungeness.

Though only two pairs actually nested, the third pair, whose nest had been accidentally destroyed, were frequently present. When first discovered both pairs were busily feeding their young, though during every week-day workmen were equally busily excavating sand for building. Additionally, up to 148 bird-watchers a day visited the site and only careful controlling by the voluntary war-dens enabled the adults to continue visiting their nests and feeding their young. Eventually on 23 September the last juvenile left the second nest and joined the flock of thirteen birds that now roamed the Sussex countryside. Two broods, of four and three, had been successfully reared and within a couple of days all were on their way. Though preparations were made to watch over the birds should they return in 1956, the doubts expressed about their poss-ible return proved to be justified. No Bee-eaters have bred in Britain since 1955.

Though it was viewed at the time as possibly being a further exam-ple of the spread of Scandinavian species into Britain, the nesting of the Bluethroat in Scotland in 1968 remains an isolated occurrence. The bird was discovered in a marshy area of Moray by J.J.D. Greenwood, S.R. Pepper, Dr M.J. Cotton and Miss G.M. Bartlett on 13 June while they were out bird-watching. It was a female and because of the late date a half-hearted and unsuccessful attempt to find a nest was made. Fortunately the party had perforce to pass through the marsh on their return about an hour later. Once again the bird was flushed and Mr Pepper found the first British Bluethroat nest at the end of a low dead branch. It contained three eggs which, as the observers themselves pointed out, could be photographed, as the Bluethroat was too rare to be protected by Schedule 1 of the Protection of Birds Act 1954–67.

The following day Miss Bartlett returned to the nest and noted the addition of a fourth egg, but no sign of the female. By 20 June she had added two more eggs and was incubating. On 14 July, by which time half-grown young could reasonably be expected to be present, the nest was deserted and only a few nibbled pieces of egg shell remained. No doubt a small mammal had been the villain. Unfortunately the male was never seen and so the actual race, that is Red-spotted or White-spotted, could not be determined. As a freak occurrence it could have been either; as part of the spread southwards and westwards of Scandinavian birds it would have been the Red-spotted.

The final member of this collection of erratic breeders is both a strange one and one whose story may not yet be finished. The Moustached Warbler is a resident of the Mediterranean region of western Europe, but a summer visitor to eastern Europe. It was added to the British List on the basis of an individual said to have been collected at St Leonards on 12 April 1915. As one of the notorious 'Hastings Rarities' this record is now unacceptable. The next record is of nothing less than breeding in Cambridgeshire in August 1946, to which we shall return. Thereafter the species was identified at Totton near Southampton on 13 August 1951, where two birds were seen; at Cliffe in north Kent on 14 April 1952; at Wendover in Buckinghamshire on 31 July 1965, when the bird was actually trapped and examined in the hand; and at Angmering in Sussex where a bird was seen on 18 August 1979.

The Cambridgeshire birds were discovered by R.A. Hinde and A.S. Thom in August 1946 and watched feeding three fledged chicks in an inaccessible part of the marsh. Their full account appeared in *British Birds* but, as that outspoken ornithologist, the late Colonel Richard Meinertzhagen, pointed out, there is nothing in it that could not equally be true of a Sedge Warbler. No doubt field identification has improved considerably since Meinertzhagen's day, when a good sighting of a bird was usually obtained along the barrel of a four-ten. The BOU List Committee accepted the record and it is included in their *Status of Birds in Britain and Ireland*.

However, in the August 1980 issue of *British Birds* both Colin Bibby and Andrew Duff pointed out that a photograph of a Moustached Warbler taken abroad in 1964 by Dr Kevin Carlson was, in their independent opinions, a Sedge Warbler. Without wishing to go into the reasons for their doubts, the point is clear. It seems unlikely that Messrs Hinde and Thom could have had better views of their birds than a photographer working a few feet from the nest. Nor is it likely that they would have enjoyed the overseas experience of Dr and Mrs Carlson. So, while Dr Carlson in his reply in *British Birds* of November 1980 affirms the identification of a Moustached Warbler as correct, the fact that such a dispute over a photograph can arise must give cause for doubt of what is, after all, an unlikely occurrence. In the circumstances it is not unreasonable to stand with Meinertzhagen (and Bannerman come to that) and say that if the Moustached Warbler has bred in Britain it remains unproven.

Here, then, is a collection of 'once in a lifetime' events in British ornithology. These 'one-offs' are the exception and there are few enough of them. With their documentation the story of our changing avifauna of breeding birds is complete. . .to date. This last proviso is important, for before this book is published, it will already be out of date. Some new bird will have bred, another may have returned, an erratic may startle some fortunate observers and make the ornithological headlines. Things are continuously changing, and it is just because they are changing that so many of us find birds, and the observation of them, fascinating.

Chapter Thirteen

The Crystal Ball

Britain's avifauna has changed, is changing, and will continue to change. Some birds have deserted us as breeding species, while others have colonized these islands for the first time. On the basis of past experience it would seem likely that this process of local extinction and colonization will continue and it is interesting to speculate as to which species might be involved.

Conservationists have learned their lessons well. Today they are concerned with conserving habitats and hope, by so doing, to conserve birds that might otherwise disappear along with them. Successful species that have learned to live alongside man will, it is safe to assume, remain with us and extend their range and increase in numbers. It seems unlikely that the twenty-first century will see a 'Save the Starling Fund', or similar funds devoted to House Sparrows, Blackbirds, or such like. Habitats that are most under threat at the moment are the most likely to disappear within the next fifty years, and with them will go several birds that seem to be declining at present. Conservationists have proved themselves quite able to protect existing, and create new, marshlands — but will they be able to protect and/or create heathlands?

British heathland is home to a select band of species that includes Stone-curlew, Red-backed Shrike, Woodlark, Nightjar, Stonechat, Whinchat and others. There has been a startling decline in the numbers of the first four of these species and perhaps also of the fifth. Yet, as we have seen, there has already been a small colonization of Red-backed Shrikes in Scotland that may compensate for the decline and, perhaps, eventual disappearance of this bird from southern England. To date there has been no hint of a matching colonization of either Woodlarks or Nightjars, species that both have a similar Scandinavian range. In the case of the Woodlark the *Atlas* population was put between 200 and 450 pairs and declining fast. In the London area, for instance, there were forty-five pairs within twenty miles of St Paul's in 1950, but none at all fourteen years later.

The ploughing of marginal land and earlier harvesting have wrought havoc on the population of the Stone-curlew. Its survival in southern England now hangs in the balance.

This decline has been reflected elsewhere, in Germany, France and the Low Countries. Though a number of different reasons have been suggested, including a bout of severe winters, the decline of the rabbit and subsequent disappearance of short-cropped grassy areas, and the deteriorating climate, the exact causes remain a mystery. Certainly, however, there is every sign that the Woodlark will disappear from England and Wales in the not-too-distant future without any compensatory colonization from the north.

As it is with the Woodlark so it is with the Nightjar. In recent years county after county has reported a decline in numbers and the *Atlas* was able to estimate the total population at only 3,000 to 6,000 pairs in 1969–72. Most of these were concentrated in southern and eastern England, where open woodland has been progressively destroyed and heathland developed or disturbed. The chances of any conservation organization being able to do anything about maintaining numbers of either Woodlarks or Nightjars must be considered slim. A holding operation that maintains a small nucleus of breeding pairs may be possible, but in the longer term and in the country as a whole their demise seems only a matter of time.

In the case of the Stone-curlew the situation seems even more desperate. From a population of between 1,000 and 2,000 pairs between the wars numbers had dropped to 300 to 500 pairs by 1970. The disappearance of heath and chalklands under the plough has undoubtedly been a major factor, as has reafforestation of much marginal land like, for instance, the East Anglian Brecks. However, the Stone-curlew does not breed in Scandinavia and cannot, therefore, mount a recolonization from the north. Gradually the species will decline and eventually cease to breed in Britain — perhaps within twenty or thirty years.

Several other species exist in Britain only in very small numbers, or in tiny restricted habitats. Red-necked Phalaropes were down to twenty-two to thirty-six pairs in 1978, yet this was by all accounts a very good year, and included a return to the Scottish mainland after an absence of several years. Corncrakes have been declining for years and are now more or less confined to the Outer Hebrides, Tiree and Ireland. They seem safe enough, but there seems little chance of their recolonizing the mainland.

Cirl Buntings, meanwhile, are contracting their range at the other end of the country. They are now virtually confined to the area south of the M4, with a population of 350 to 700 pairs, whereas they were formerly regular as far away as North Wales. Being resident they are particularly prone to severe winters and there can be little doubt that climatic change is the main cause of the decline.

Much the same can be said of the Dartford Warbler, a heathland species particularly prone to harsh weather conditions. Heathland continues to disappear and every hard winter sees the numbers of this little warbler reduced to virtually nil. Yet somehow a few do manage to survive and within a few brief years numbers build up dramatically once more. Even a succession of two very severe winters, as in 1962 and 1963, which included the longest spell of freezing this century, failed to wipe the Dartford Warbler out completely. So, perhaps, there may be less cause for alarm about this species whose population rarely exceeds five hundred and which may be (on occasion) virtually Britain's rarest breeding bird, than about others that seem to be slowly, but inexorably, disappearing. These, then, are the most likely losses, but which species are most likely to take their places?

Writing, or rather lecturing, in 1971, J. Ferguson-Lees listed fourteen species as possible colonists or recolonists: Purple Heron, Spoonbill, Turnstone, Broad-billed Sandpiper, Jack Snipe, Long-tailed Skua, Little Gull, Shore Lark, Cetti's Warbler, Great Reed Warbler, Bonelli's Warbler, Great Grey Shrike, Scarlet Rosefinch and Ortolan Bunting. Within ten years Little Gull, Shore Lark and Cetti's Warbler had all bred and several of the others seem distinct possibilities to do so. However, there are several other species that seem even more likely to colonize.

In general, the increasing occurrence of birds as visitors is no indication of the likelihood or not of breeding. There are, for example, more reports of Pectoral Sandpipers than Spotted Sandpipers, but while the latter has bred the former has not. An increase in the number of vagrants may be an indication of increasing population or extension of range, but it would seem to be much more fruitful to look at range extensions actually taking place in the adjacent areas of the Continent, rather than their possible effects on the number of vagrants occurring in Britain. Melodious Warblers may be much more numerous as vagrants than, say, Red-rumped Swallows, but I would guess that the Swallow is a more likely colonist because it is extending its range rapidly northwards by occupying newly-created nest sites. From southern Spain in the mid-1950s Red-rumped Swallows moved northwards and westwards as far as the Costa Brava by the late 1960s. Within ten years they had extended along the Mediterranean coast into France and had started pushing northwards. Most nests are found on concrete structures, such as bridges and uncompleted buildings, sites that were unknown only fifty years ago. Being summer visitors with an increasing propensity to overshoot their breeding range in spring, they would seem to be very likely candidates to colonize Britain within the next twenty or thirty years.

Another strong contender is the Penduline Tit, which is spreading westwards across northern Europe and which has colonized

Denmark and adjacent parts of northern Germany in the last twenty-five years. The bird has the distinction of having been added to the Dutch Check-List before it was seen in that country. A cock bird was present during the breeding season and constructed a nest that was discovered by Dutch ornithologists only after the bird had disappeared. On the basis of the nest the Penduline Tit was added to the Dutch List. The species was first added to the British List in 1966, but was not seen again until 1978. No doubt as the range extends along the southern shores of the North Sea, vagrants will become progressively more frequent in their occurrence. One day, perhaps next century, someone will discover a nest in Britain.

From the same direction Tengmalm's Owl may eventually arrive. There is some evidence of a westward extension of range in France and the species was first recorded in Holland in 1971. From 1973 onwards it was noted annually and breeding was finally confirmed in 1977. This may, of course, be no more than an isolated occurrence, but there are now several breeding records from Belgium, near the Luxembourg border.

Several other 'southern' birds may be considered as possible British colonizers. Syrian Woodpeckers crossed into Europe in 1890, reached central Europe in the 1960s and were into Austria by 1971. The Olivaceous Warbler, extending its range in a north-westerly direction, had reached Vienna by 1967. At present rates of progress both species should arrive in Britain in the first quarter of the twenty-first century.

Despite persistent rumours there is no satisfactory record of Little Bittern nesting in Britain. Though there seems every chance of its doing so (a male was reported calling during the summer of 1970 and a pair were present in 1979), there nevertheless seems little likelihood of its improving on its erratic status with us, and becoming a regular breeder.

In contrast a veritable population explosion has affected the diminutive Fan-tailed Warbler, perhaps better called Zitting Cisticola in line with world usage. Confined to the shores of the Mediterranean in the mid-1950s, this dull-looking bird with the distinctive voice and song-flight has colonized larger and larger areas of Europe in recent years. It has spread northwards up the French Atlantic coast and thence eastwards along the Channel coast. It has already colonized the island of Crete, so lengthy water

Next on the list? It seems only a matter of time before some fortunate observer hears the 'zip-zip-zip' call of the Fan-tailed Warbler and discovers its nest in southern England.

crossings are no handicap, and three individuals appeared in Britain between 1973 and 1977, the last one in song at Lodmoor in Dorset. At the time of writing it is poised no further away than Boulogne — its arrival in Britain can only be a matter of time.

One of the features of the 1970s was, as we have seen, the colonization of species from the north. From Scandinavia came Redwings and Fieldfares, Bramblings and Bluethroats, Temminck's Stints and Wood Sandpipers, Shore Larks and Purple Sandpipers. In this area we have an established pattern of colonization, a colonization that also brought the Wryneck to Scotland, just as it was about to withdraw from England. Clearly, then, Scandinavia should prove a happy hunting ground for the student of potential British colonists. However, a word of warning. Several of these northern colonists, some of which seemed perfectly well

Will the Turnstone be the next Scandinavian bird to colonize Scotland? Many think it will, and some believe it already breeds on some low, grassy, offshore holm.

established only a few years ago, have already withdrawn. This may indicate the end of such colonizations or perhaps only a stage along the way. Certainly Scandinavia offers several other distinct possibilities including the Turnstone, perhaps the prime candidate. Turnstones breed along all Scandinavian coasts and would find a plentiful supply of suitable offshore islands around Scotland. They are regular winter visitors in good numbers and have often stayed on late in spring to the excitement of many Scottish observers.

Other Scandinavian waders do not breed so close, but several must be counted as potential colonists of the far north. The Broad-billed Sandpiper is a rare visitor to our shores, with a southerly rather than south-westerly autumn migration route. But it breeds as far south as the Hardangervidda in Norway, an area also favoured by Wood and Purple Sandpipers and Temminck's Stint, all of which have colonized Scotland in recent years. Also possibles are Green Sandpiper, Jack Snipe and Great Snipe, which have a sub-Arctic distribution. Other species with a solid Scandinavian range include Velvet Scoter, Spotted Redshank, Long-tailed Skua, Great Grey Shrike, Ortolan Bunting and Long-tailed Duck. The latter may well have bred on a couple of occasions last century in Shetland and in Orkney in 1911. Breeding was suspected in the Outer Hebrides in 1969 and pairs are regularly seen elsewhere in Scotland in summer. Which, if any, of these can be expected to breed in the future is, however, pure guesswork, but interesting for all that.

Yet another group of colonists, if that is the correct term in this case, are the accidental introductions — birds that have escaped from collections and established a feral breeding population. Already established in this category, though still not admitted to the British List, are the Black-crowned Night-Herons that have flown in and out of the grounds of Edinburgh Zoo since 1950. The Red-crested Pochards that breed at Frampton-on-Severn doubtless had their origins at the Wildfowl Trust's grounds at adjacent Slimbridge. Reeves's Pheasants breed in a number of different areas and it can only be a matter of time before they join Golden and Lady Amherst's Pheasants on the official list. Bobwhite Quails breed near Minsmere and on Tresco in the Isles of Scilly, but their status must be considered far from secure. They seemed well established in Norfolk between 1820 and 1845, but were then eliminated by a succession of severe winters.

Though the list of potential breeders that have escaped from captivity includes such diverse species as Budgerigar, Canary, Java Sparrow and Pin-tailed Whydah, there is evidence of successful colonization only by one true exotic — the Rose-ringed Parakeet. From escapes or releases in 1969–70 these attractive and gregarious birds have established themselves in several south London suburbs, as well as in Kent and Sussex. In 1979 I saw a bird at Westleton in Suffolk, not a mile from the RSPB's reserve at Minsmere.

Inevitably, however, it is natural change that provokes the most interest and speculation among bird-watchers. A new bird that finds its own way over the seas to colonize our countryside for the first time has a romance about it that no introduction or escape could ever match. At the time of writing bird-watchers in northern Scotland and in the extreme south-east of England seem to have the best chances of discovering a new breeder — in the south they will be looking out for Fan-tailed Warblers, in the north perhaps for Long-tailed Ducks and Turnstones.

FURTHER READING

Abbey, George. *The Balance of Nature*. London, 1909.

Bannerman, D.A. and Lodge, G.E. *The Birds of the British Isles*. 12 vols. 1953–63.

Baxter, E.V. and Rintoul, L.J. *The Birds of Scotland*. Edinburgh, 1953.

Bijleveld, Maarten. *Birds of Prey in Europe*. London, 1974.

Booth, E.T. *Rough Notes*. 1881–7.

Booth, E.T. *Catalogue of the Cases of Birds in Dyke Road Museum, Brighton*. 1876.

British Birds. Rare Breeding Birds. Reports, various years.

British Ornithologists' Union. *The Status of Birds in Britain and Ireland*. Oxford, 1971.

Brown, Leslie. *British Birds of Prey*. London, 1976.

Brown, P. *Avocets in England*. RSPB, 1950.

Brown, Philip and Waterston, George. *The Return of the Osprey*. London, 1962.

Browne, Sir Thomas. *Account of Birds found in Norfolk and Suffolk*. 1682.

Cameron of Lochiel. Recollections about the Ospreys at Achnacarry. *British Birds* (magazine). 1943.

Chapman, Abel. *Birds of the Borders*. London, 1889.

Darby, Frank Fraser. *Natural History in the Highlands and Islands*. London, 1947.

Fisher, James. *The Fulmar*. London, 1952.

Fisher, James. The Collared Turtle Dove in Europe. *British Birds* (magazine). 1953.

Fisher, James and Lockley, R.M. *Seabirds*. London, 1954.

Fisher, James. *The Shell Bird Book*. London, 1966.

Gladstone, H. *Shooting Bags and Shooting Records*. 1922.

Gooders, John (Editor). *Birds of the World*. London, 1969–71.

Graham, Henry Davenport. *The Birds of Iona and Mull*. Edinburgh, 1890.

Gray, Robert. *Birds of the West of Scotland*. 1871.

Gurney, J.H. *Catalogue of a Collection of British Birds*. 1892.

Harvie-Brown, J.A. and Buckley, T.E. *A Vertebrate Fauna of the Moray Basin*. 2 vols. Edinburgh, 1812; *A Vertebrate Fauna of Sutherland, Caithness and West Cromarty*. Edinburgh, 1887; *A Vertebrate Fauna of the Outer Hebrides*. Edinburgh, 1888; *A Vertebrate Fauna of the Inner Hebrides*. Edinburgh, 1892.

Harvie-Brown, J.A. and Macpherson, the Reverend H.A. *A Vertebrate*

Fauna of the North-west Highlands and Skye. Edinburgh, 1904.

Harvie-Brown, J.A. *A Vertebrate Fauna of the Tay Basin*. Edinburgh, 1906.

Jardine, Sir William. *Birds of Great Britain and Ireland*. Naturalists' Library. London, 1838–42.

Johns, the Reverend C.A. *British Birds in Their Haunts*. London, 1910.

Lodge, R.B. *Bird Hunting Through Wild Europe*. London, 1912.

Macgillivray, William. *Descriptions of the Rapacious Birds of Great Britain*. London, 1836.

Macgillivray, William. *History of British Birds*. London, 1837–52.

Payn, William, H. *The Birds of Suffolk*. London, 1962.

Pennant, T. *A Tour in Scotland and Voyage to the Outer Hebrides*. 1771–6.

Pennant, T. *British Zoology*. 1812.

Rivière, B.B. *A History of the Birds of Norfolk*. London, 1930.

Royce, Robert. *Breviary of Suffolk*. 1618.

Seago, M.J. *Birds of Norfolk*. Norwich, 1967.

Sharrock, J.T.R. *The Atlas of Breeding Birds in Britain and Ireland*. Tring, 1976.

Smith, the Reverend Alfred. *Birds of Wiltshire*. 1878.

St John, Charles William. *Natural History and Sport in Moray*. 1863.

St John, Charles William. *A Tour of Sutherland*. 1849.

Stanford, J.K. In *Avocets in England* by Philip Brown, RSPB, 1950.

INDEX